CW01572964

A Guide to Developing a Retention and Disposal Schedule for Business Information

Contents

Acknowledgements

This Guide has been prepared under the authority of, and through the sponsorship of, the BSI Freedom of Information and Data Protection Editorial Boards. BSI would like to thank representatives of the following authoritative bodies for their contributions:

Group 5;

UKAIIM Standards Committee;

Elizabeth Barber   Records Management Society –
Local Government Group.

UKAIIM Standards Committee Acknowledgements

Rob Allen	e-Bv e-business process visualisation
Keith Batchelor	Batchelor Associates
Cimtech	
Marc Fresko	Cornwell Management Consultants plc
Rana Ghosh-Roy	
Chris Hayden	Anacomp Document Solutions
Andy Pibworth	Chairman UKAIIM Standards Committee
Alan Shipman	Group 5 Training Ltd

Preface

This Guide has been written to inform records managers, senior company executives and other managers at all levels about the need for retention scheduling and the advantages it provides. It is designed to assist in the production of a suitable retention schedule for use under the Data Protection Act 1998 and the Freedom of Information Act 2000, both of which can have an effect on organisations from small enterprises to those with a global presence. Such a retention policy (i.e. the broad objectives covering the reasons for having a schedule, who authorized it, who has the delegated powers to maintain the schedule on a day-to-day basis, and how it relates to the records management policy) and schedule (i.e. details on information held and for how long, etc.) should be part of the overall records management policy.

This book takes the reader step-by-step through the process of developing a retention schedule, from finding out what information is held by their organization to producing a suitable schedule. A flow chart that follows the order of the paragraphs is included for guidance.

Advice and sample forms on questionnaires, methods, layouts, destruction and archiving with the pros and cons of the different methods that may be employed are provided.

Information on the actual retention timeframes is based on research of over 200,000 pages of legislation (including Acts and Statutory Instruments), codes of practice and the author's experience.

In following the advice within the Guide, the reader will be starting to comply with BS ISO 15489-1:2001 (8.3.7 and 9.2), BS ISO 15489-2:2001 (4.2.4.3), the code of practice on records management from the Lord Chancellor and the advice of the Information Commissioners for England, Wales and Scotland. All of these mention the need for a retention and disposal policy in order to show compliance with current legislation.

It is not the intention of this Guide to lay down guidance on all records management practices, although some are mentioned to help the reader understand the content of this book. If additional knowledge on records management is required then it is recommended that the reader consult BS 5454 and BS ISO 15489 (both parts), or contact one of the following:

- The Records Management Society of Great Britain;

- The Society of Archivists;

- UK AIIM Standards Committee.

Contact details can be found in Appendix I.

Retention schedule flowchart

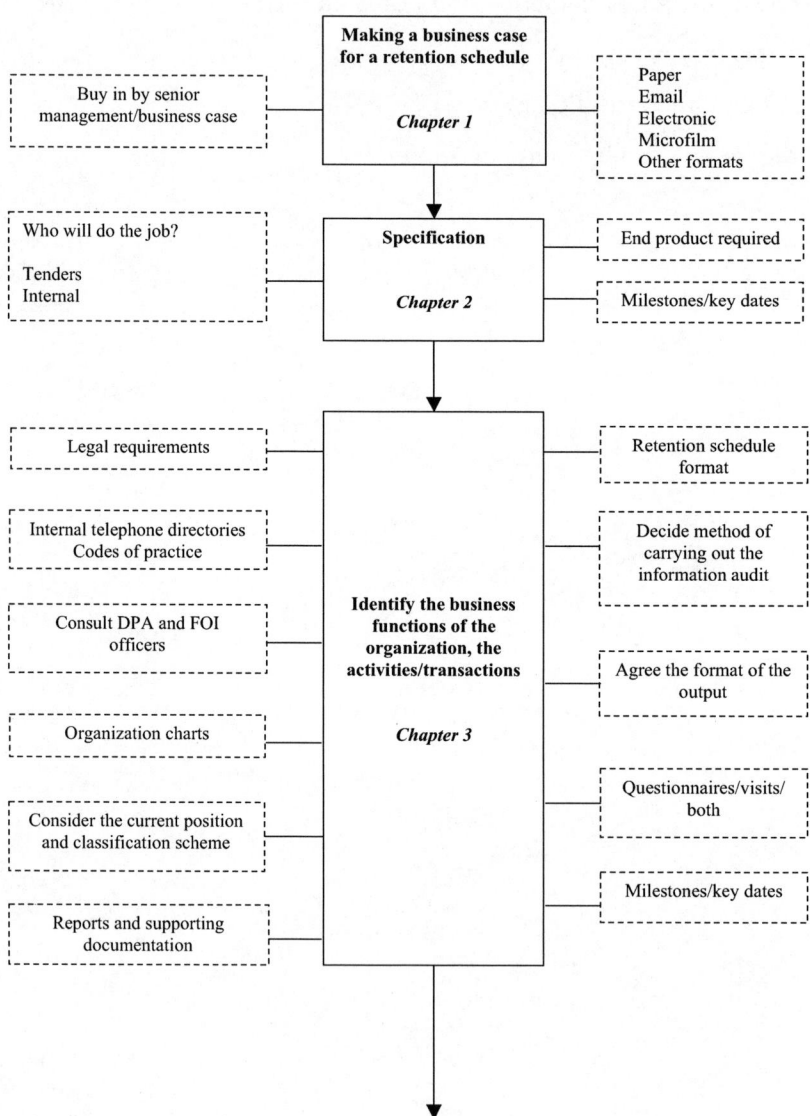

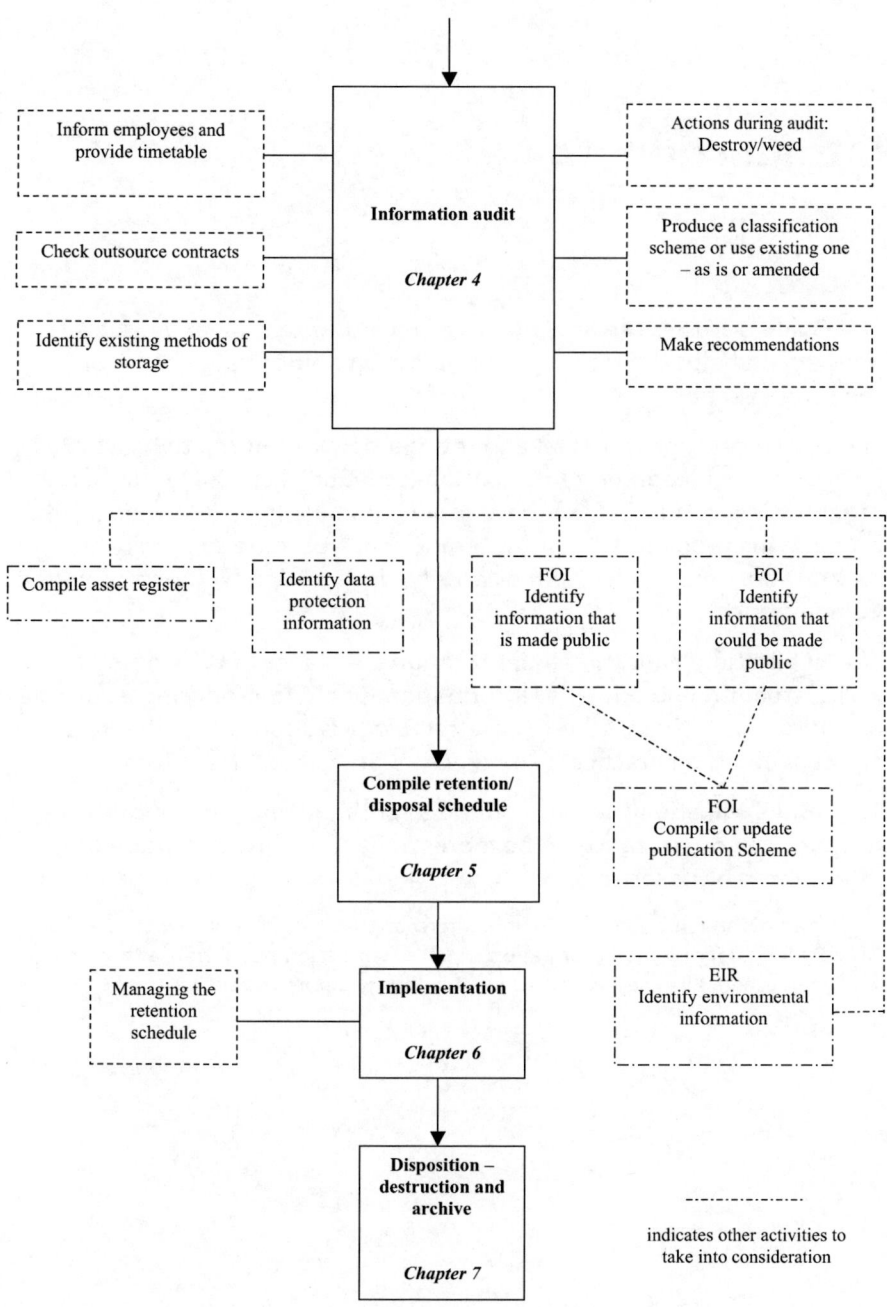

indicates other activities to
take into consideration

Introduction

This Guide discusses the advantages of records retention and disposal policies and helps the reader to formulate an appropriate policy for their organization.

The Data Protection Act 1998 and the Freedom of Information Act 2000 (including the Freedom of Information (Scotland) Act 2002) both require organizations to put in place a retention schedule in order to carry out properly the requirements of the legislation. Not to do so leaves the organization open to criticism or possible legal action by the Information Commissioner.

This publication leads the reader through the stages of developing a policy, from finding out what information is held to producing a suitable retention and disposal schedule. Terminology is kept to a minimum and advice is based on practical experience, as are the specimen forms.

The results will also assist with business continuity management, thus enabling the organization to be more resilient against disruption or interruption of its services.

NOTE: records and information are used interchangeably in this publication (see the Glossary for a definition of information). Quoted legislation was correct at the time of writing but should be checked with a legal authority before relying on it.

Chapter 1 – Making a business case for a retention schedule

What is a retention schedule?

A retention schedule, or more accurately a retention and disposal schedule, governs the retention and disposal of information generated during the daily business of an organization. It is essential for the smooth running of an efficient records management system. It ensures continuity, protects the organization's legal rights and preserves information for the archives.

Why do we need one?

There are savings to be made by only keeping information for as long as is necessary. To do so for longer can incur costs, just as disposing of the information too soon can incur penalties. Therefore it is in the interest of the chief executive or the board to be appraised of the advantages of knowing just what information is being held, together with the advantages of having an up-to-date retention schedule. The former will enable your organization to make informed decisions and policy based on current and historical facts, enhancing the performance of activities or functions of the organization.

A retention schedule will help you comply with statutory or regulatory requirements such as the Data Protection Act, protect the organization against litigation, or indeed support litigation against others by retaining information for as long as it is needed through a good regular business practice.

In summary, organizations will be able to prove compliance with legal and audit requirements, protect the interests of the business, prove integrity, and improve availability and traceability, as well as save on staff time and company costs.

Case study – National Library of Scotland

I discovered from our audit that we can get rid of 255 linear metres of redundant paper. I have also identified areas where our DPA compliance was at possible risk. And the audit enabled the creation of the Library's first ever corporate business classification scheme, which will have all sorts of positive spin offs. Not to mention uncovering some 'lost gems'. It took twice as long as I originally estimated, but I feel really confident about the decisions that I have made based on the audit. Because I am able to explain how much space I need for a proper archive and records centre, management have identified a really excellent space. It will mean I can be more engaged with the documents and my work, so I am also benefiting.

Corporate Information Officer, National Library of Scotland.

The importance of records/information retention and disposal

The average office worker files 2,000 documents (taking up to half a square metre of space in a traditional filing system) every year. At a rental rate per square metre of £200 every year, this soon mounts up.

... The number one cause of overspend in storage is the 'Blanket Policy'. Fearful of being penalised for insufficient retention, companies fail to discriminate, storing every document for up to fifty years, regardless of its importance. We estimate that 20–40 per cent of our new client's documents could be safely destroyed. The return on investment of undertaking the records classification and retention process is typically between 12 and 18 months.

Source: Iron Mountain *Information Management & Technology*, Vol. 38, No. 4, p.171.

A retention schedule:

- supports the records retention and disposal policy (which should be part of the records management strategy);
- frees up manual storage space by removing unnecessary information;

- frees up storage space on hard drives and servers by removing unnecessary data, saving on purchase and administration costs (e.g. back up, clean up, migration, etc.);

- improves access to current records, as those not required have been disposed of and there is less information to search through;

- legitimizes destruction of information (Freedom of Information, Data Protection, Tax Management Act, etc.);

- can save on staff costs, as they do not have to spend so much time searching;

- ensures that the correct information receives the appropriate level of protection.

The reasons an organization needs to retain records or information, and the corresponding benefit of having a retention schedule are:

- to comply with statutory or regulatory requirements. Only holding the appropriate information to meet the requirement keeps storage costs to a minimum;

- to protect against or support litigation. The organization has the appropriate information to support its case, again keeping storage costs to a minimum and making finding the information easier and quicker;

- to provide a corporate memory and to document an organization's activities and decisions. This saves 're-inventing the wheel' as well helping future researchers;

- to support policy formulation and decision making. Retained information will show why those decisions were made and possibly the events leading up to them, thus enabling better performance of activities or functions of the organization.

On the other hand, there are many reasons why information should be thrown away.

- Legislation such as the Data Protection Act 1998, Principle 5 – personal data processed for any purpose or purposes shall not be kept for longer than is necessary for that purpose or those purposes.

- If you still have the records, you may need to produce them (for example, there have been several court cases or tribunals where organizations have had to produce, regardless of cost, information they thought they had 'destroyed'). This could cause embarrassment and a penalty.

- It costs money to store information, in terms of floor space, disk space, and also the administration time in reviewing, weeding and searching – both for correctly filed information and misfiled information.

- It cuts down on misfiles. With less information stored it is easier to put it back in the correct place.

- It takes administrative effort to manage and search for stored files. This means a cost in staff time.

- Wasted space costs money. It could be used to store information currently sitting on desks or the floor. It reduces the time the electronic backup runs.

- There is less electronic information to migrate (BIP 0008-1, *Legal admissibility and evidential weight of information stored electronically* gives details and advice). When updating or migrating electronic information it is not cost- or time-effective to store information that will never be used.

Case study – Three organizations' approach to keeping records

- **Organization A** retains all information.

It likes to keep everything. Its lack of a retention schedule is accompanied by a lack of awareness of the need to manage information and thus risks losing all its information, accidentally or because of a disaster. So not only is organization A taking an increased business risk with its information, it is unaware of the cost of keeping and managing it.

- **Organization B** manages information on an ad-hoc basis.

From time to time it discovers that it has a large quantity of information, for which there is less and less space available. Each time space (or some other 'driver') becomes scarce, it takes a one-off decision to throw away its oldest information, in the hope that no problems will materialize. Sometimes a policy for some of the information exists, but no-one is responsible for its implementation, or the person who is responsible just moves the information to another 'hidden' store, just in case.

> • **Organization C** has an approved retention and disposal policy.
>
> It knows what information it is holding, has categorized its information, and has looked into the requirements for keeping it. It is aware of how long its information needs to be kept, and the reasons for keeping it. There is also an authorized individual who is responsible for each type of information, and who implements the disposal procedures (destruction, transfer to an archive, etc.) once the retention period has expired. The actual arrangements are shown in a retention and disposal schedule.

Only organization C has its information under control and is able to reap the benefits.

A good business plan will result in the chief executive's or the board's approval, together with the funds to carry the scheme through. This will be of great advantage when dealing with reluctant employees who have other priorities.

Who is the best person to prepare the business case? Not every organization has a records officer, especially a trained one. There may be a person with an interest in record keeping. It might be the accommodation officer tasked with the job of finding space for additional staff.

In costing the exercise you will need to check on what needs to be done from the following sections and enter the appropriate figures. Such costs will of course differ from organization to organization, depending on the size of the organization, the persons involved and time scales.

Chapter 2 – Specifications

Designing and compiling a retention schedule is not easy, being time consuming in both research and compilation. A specimen retention schedule for a typical local authority may run to over 200 pages.

In the case of health and safety alone there are over 80 Acts and over 700 Statutory Instruments that may contain reference to retention of information – some in a specified format. There are also numerous codes of practice. The Regulatory Reform (Fire Safety) Order 2005 has 12 such codes of practice and there are many others covering a variety of subjects.

There are five main ways of developing your retention and disposal schedule.

1. **Do it solely on your own.** This may take a considerable time – possibly years – but ensures it is completed to your standards. You will need the resources to read legislation and codes of practice, as well as some legal knowledge. You may need an expert to check the finished work.

2. **Delegate the task to someone else in the organization.** This needs a tight specification and good monitoring to meet your specification and timetable. You will need the time to answer questions and check the work. Again you may need an expert to check the finished work.

3. **Employ an outside consultant.** This needs a good specification and a consultant knowledgeable in records management, the business activity, statutory and other regulatory needs. It may be costly – from £300 per day. Results are likely to be available in a reasonable time scale.

4. **Copy it from another organization** (for example, the Records Management Society website: http://www.rms-gb.org.uk). Some organizations may have copyright protection and permission may be needed. It may have more or less items then you need, so may need to be amended to fit your circumstances. It may not be up to date, but could provide a broad starting point.

5. Form a committee. Several organizations have tried this approach. It requires very specific objectives and rules laid down to ensure that consistency and time scales are met and personal preferences are not forced on others. This is not to say that people should not be consulted. In fact the more people are involved with the process then the more likely they will accept the finished result and put it into practice.

Whatever method is used, an appropriate specification needs to be drawn up giving sufficient information in the tender for the potential consultant to make an informed bid. (Even if the job is kept in-house it should still have a specification.)

The following areas are useful in allowing a consultant to consider your requirements properly.

- The size of the organization in terms of the number of employees.

- The activity or business of the organization. Is this expected to change during the contract? (See Chapter 3 for further assistance in this area.)

- Will each employee be interviewed, or only managers?

- Will only certain teams or business functions be involved at this stage? If so how many are there? Can you list them?

- The time scale, including milestones and key dates. Are they negotiable?

These points give clues to the type of manpower resources that may be required.

Further areas to consider include the following.

- Is there an existing classification scheme?

- Is the consultant expected to draw up a retention schedule just from an existing classification scheme without taking an audit of what information is actually held?

- Is there an existing retention schedule?

- How much detail do you want in the retention schedule? (See Chapter 5 on compiling a retention schedule.) Do you want the results in paper or electronic form?

- How you would like any recommendations presented. For example, in a written report, electronic presentation, verbal report, spreadsheets, floppy disc or CD.

- Is the job to be done in stages?

- Do you require a storage audit to be carried out at the same time to prevent employees getting upset over 'yet another questionnaire/ interview', if such an audit follows shortly after an information audit?

Above all, give the consultant a reasonable time to reply. Often very short time scales are given for the return of a tender. The person sending out the tender may be under pressure from others within the organization, but receiving a tender on a Monday for a reply by 5 p.m. on a Friday is not good for the consultant or your organization. It can lead to bad feeling and insufficient thought and justification being given to the task, with the possible result that after the award of contract, further negotiations have to take place regarding time scales and costs. This does not place either side in a good light. A minimum of two weeks is reasonable – four weeks is better. It also gives those tendering a chance to clarify points they are not sure about and for the organization to send the answer to all recipients of the tender in order to treat all fairly.

Remember that asking for degrees as qualifications does not always get the best consultant. In the records management field there are many who have years of experience, but have no degree in the subject. The current degree courses are relatively new and places few. You need to ask for evidence of past clients and the nature of the consultancy to match your expectations.

If the task is being carried out in-house by an employee the above points still need serious thought if the employee is to carry out the task efficiently in a reasonable time scale and not waste time and money.

Chapter 3 – Business functions, activities and transactions

Information is a valuable asset and needs to be well managed.

A recent study conducted by PricewaterhouseCoopers found that professionals spend 5 to 15 per cent of their time reading information but up to 50 per cent of their time looking for pertinent data.

The average organization also:

- makes 19 copies of each document it receives or produces;

- loses 1 out of every 20 documents;

- spends 25 hours recreating each lost document; and

- spends 400 hours per year searching for lost files.

Whether your auditor is an external consultant or an internal employee, they need to understand the way the organization operates. This may have been in the specification but it is worth checking that they really know what the business does. What are the business functions of the organization? What departments operate within the organization (e.g. customer services, finance, human resources, health and safety, transport)?

Talk to the data protection officer and the freedom of information (FOI) officer. (Sometimes these are combined, or the records officer may have these duties as well.) This will help to identify the activities and transactions of the organization at an operational level, since these persons will have day-to-day experience with much of the information in order to fulfil their statutory duties. Relevant codes of practice and legal requirements appropriate to the type of business being run will also contain valuable information regarding what should be retained and for how long.

Identify and collect relevant background documentation, which is likely to include:

- an organization chart showing departments and personnel from the CEO downwards;
- possibly an information management strategy and policy framework;
- an information management implementation plan;
- the most recent information survey carried out within the organization;
- current retention and disposal guidance;
- internal telephone directories and floor plans. These will also give an idea of how the organization operates.

In addition your initial research should include the following:

- the current classifications being used and whether they fit the current business functions. If not, find out why. (See Chapter 4 regarding action on this point after the audit results are known.);
- any similar work undertaken to date, the current position and any additional research currently planned;
- contact details for the nominated officers with whom you will be working;
- a list of which individuals are to be consulted during the assignment with their contact details. These are likely to include representatives of the key high-level business functions.

Confirm the agreement on the format of the project output, even though it may have been included in the original specification, particularly the layout of the retention schedule and explanatory or supporting documentation that make up the system and any other documentation that may be required.

Should the citations be part of the retention schedule or do you require them to be listed separately, either on paper or in a spreadsheet? Even such things as the size of paper and whether landscape or portrait layout should be used have been known to change after the tender has been awarded. Time spent at this stage can save time and money as well as avoid disagreements and disappointments.

Chapter 4 – The information audit

> **Who owns the information created at work?**
>
> Under copyright ownership and moral rights, the default owner is the person who created the work, **unless the work was completed in the course of employment.**

Just as a company will carry out a stocktake from time to time to ensure the goods held match the theory figures, so organizations should carry out a stocktake or audit of the information they hold.

To achieve this successfully it must be made clear to employees from the top downwards that information gained through the activities of the business belongs to the business and not to an individual or department. This kind of audit has been given various names, such as records census, records survey, information audit or record inventory to name but a few. In this publication we use the term 'information audit'.

There are various ways of finding out what information is held, where it is held, why it is held and by whom.

- **Questionnaire** (See Appendix A for a sample and explanation of each question.)

  A questionnaire may be given to the manager of a department or to each individual employee. The questionnaire needs careful design, with wording everyone understands, and should be as short as possible. Sometimes a sheet of notes or explanation is included. It need not be in paper format. It could be posted on the intranet.

  In theory it saves the time of the auditor but in practice the questionnaire rarely gets completed on time and in full. The auditor then has to visit each department, section or person to complete the task from scratch.

- **Personal visits**

Personal visits can be time consuming, especially if employees fail to keep appointments or allow the interview to be interrupted by phone calls or visitors. It is, however, a more accurate method, and gives the auditor the chance to see for themselves the type of information held and to ask questions (preferably of the open type, as opposed to closed questions that just need yes or no for an answer). There is also the chance to provide some advice or for the employee to ask questions.

- **Combination of both of the above**

Questionnaires may be sent out beforehand and the auditor studies the results before visiting to ask any further questions. In practice this also gives the employee a chance to clear out unneeded information (such as magazines, old telephone directories, etc.) before the auditor arrives! This combination technique is usually the quickest and most effective, as well as being efficient. Employees do need to be informed that the auditor will be arriving to discuss incomplete or unclear questionnaires!

Timetable and method of informing employees

Whichever method you choose, staff need to be informed about the work you are going to undertake. This can be done in various ways (although a personal approach is likely to be more effective):

- global email;
- presentations at team meetings;
- briefing senior managers who cascade the information to their teams;
- briefing notes;
- workshops and seminars;
- staff newsletters;
- intranet.

It is essential that such communications emphasise the senior management's commitment. The chief executive could supply a statement showing his commitment and stating who within the organization will be organizing the audit on their behalf. If the individual members of staff are not fully informed, the audit will take longer than it should and/or will not be completed properly. Members of staff also need to be reassured that the information audit is not being undertaken to downsize numbers of staff (unless this is the case), but to reduce the amount of information held, aid its quick retrieval, and help it flow around the organization – and so make their job easier.

An outline timetable should be drawn up so employees know when the auditor is due to visit. Although this sounds fundamental, in reality it often does not happen. It should also be explained to them how much time will be needed for the interview and that it would be beneficial to both parties if the interview was not interrupted by telephone calls or visitors. Just as some interviewees will welcome auditors with open arms and be in awe of their advice, others will resent giving even a minute of their time. This is where charm, diplomacy and the backing of the chief executive come into play.

The information audit – questions to be asked

See Appendix A for a specimen questionnaire.

- What is the information?
- Why is it being retained – what is its purpose?
- How is kept? (Format/storage)
- Who holds the information?
- Who is responsible for the information?
- Where is it being kept?
- How should it be protected?
- How is the information used? (By one person, by several, across the organization?)
- Who else holds copies? Which is the master copy?
- When should it be destroyed or transferred to the archives?
- How should it be destroyed?
- Is it affected by the Freedom of Information Act 2000 or the Data Protection Act 1998 or the Environmental Information Regulations 2004?

There needs to be an audit of *all* the information held to ensure a complete list is available. This will include all media types (e.g. paper, film and electronic) and in some cases 'hard' objects such as drill core samples or evidence required for production in courts.

Copies held in personal files kept by individuals in notebooks and desk drawers should be taken into consideration, as should copies of electronic data held on back-up media, hard drives, floppies, flash drives, laptops, videos, CCTV and CDs. This includes files marked 'personal' or 'miscellaneous' if they contain information about the organization. The organization's records management policy should spell out this point in order for it not to fall foul of data protection legislation. If it does not then the organization needs to consult site unions and human resources on an agreed policy for monitoring and auditing information held by the organization.

Many employees have a 'personal file'. In some cases it may indeed be personal, with information only about themselves; in other cases it holds information to do with the organization but only relevant to them or their managers. *Anything produced during the course of employment belongs to the employer.* The notes made at meetings or on sticky notes belong to the employer. Any drafts or 'just in case' back-ups held on the hard drive belong to the organization. Information copied on to flash drives or laptops for working at home belongs to the employer. Contents of emails are not personal if sent in work time on work equipment. The employer may allow some latitude in this, but as they will be liable in law for the content should it be abusive, pornographic or racist then the contents cannot be truly personal. 'Personal' emails and paper notes should be just that – dental appointments, lunch appointments, etc. and destroyed as soon as they have been actioned.

Even reference books such as telephone directories should be checked to ensure the latest edition is being used. All material held should be considered, including old trade magazines, which should not be kept unless they contain relevant up-to-date reference material. Similarly, old office circulars and similar documents need not be retained if a master set is kept by the human resources department.

The IT department can supply a list of databases and users. It will also help establish links and identify possible data protection issues: one database on its own may not fall under the Data Protection Act 1998, but if two or more can be linked then they may identify a data subject and as such should be notified to the Information Commissioner.

According to Alison Gibney, Senior Consultant at Cimtech Ltd, as a guide, an information audit will take around one day for every 25 staff: perhaps a year of one person's full-time effort for a large organization. You should set a deadline of three weeks after the audit, by which all responses must be returned. Allow another week or so after this for stragglers. You need to formulate a method of collating the responses into a spreadsheet. A county council or government department may produce 1,000 responses and copying and pasting will be a slow process.

Information storage

Such an audit could also be used to identify the types of storage in use to see if the information is being kept in an efficient manner. Consider the following.

- Could paper be scanned or filmed for faster access, reduced storage or back-up purposes?

- Would storage in a linear form be more beneficial than using filing cabinets and use less storage space?

- Can fixed shelving be replaced by mobile shelving?

- Is storing off site a cheaper option?

Combining the information and storage audits saves time and prevents employees being bothered by yet another survey.

The physical location for the storage of each record should be identified and documented. For physical records such as paper and microfilm, this may be a shelf location, a box number or filing cabinet. For electronic files, storage space on servers (for online storage) or storage devices (jukeboxes, tape libraries, etc.) will need to be identified and allocated.

As a rule of thumb, between 30 per cent and 60 per cent of information can usually be destroyed if no such audit has taken place in the previous five years or more.

Even if the person or persons carrying out the audit know the site well, it is still a good idea to have a floor plan with all the furniture marked so areas can be marked off when complete. Coloured pens are invaluable for doing this especially when sections are in different parts of the floor or some distance from their storage facility. In some organizations the cupboards are all in the centre of the floor and in others in a separate room or even on a different floor! It helps to link relevant information and people together to ensure nothing has been missed.

Where storage or record facilities are outsourced then a copy of the contract or agreement needs to be studied to find out what is being handled, who is handling it and who is responsible for retention, disposition and destruction decisions. It may be the company storing the information. The auditor's recommendations may well end up being in conflict with the contract. Is there a get-out clause? Is the organization able to specify retention schedules to the storage company? How long has the contract to run? It has been known for organizations to forget to inform the storage company of their updated retention schedule and end up paying for the storage of information no longer required.

The entire information gained can be presented in a variety of ways, such as a table or a spreadsheet. Consider to whom you are making your report or presentation. What was specified in your remit?

Recommendations

At the end of the audit the results can be reviewed and the following recommendations may be made depending on whether just an information audit was carried out, or a storage one as well.

Recommendations following an information audit

- Confirmation that the existing classification scheme is suitable or, if not, where changes might be made.

- Which information needs to be retained.

- Which information may be disposed of.

- Which information needs to be protected by back-ups.

- Which information needs a security classification or should be locked away when not in use.

- What may fall under the Data Protection Act 1998 or the Environmental Information Regulations 2004.

- What might be exempt under the Freedom of Information Act 2000.

- Whether any workflow systems could be improved.

Recommendations following a storage audit

- Which electronic information should be migrated to allow access by new software or hardware (BIP 0008, *Code of Practice for Legal Admissibility*).

- Which information should be in fire-resistant safes or data safes. (Data safes have a greater heat resistance and should be used for the storage of electronic and film data, as these are more susceptible to fire at lower temperatures than paper.)

- How the information is accessed and how often.

- By how much the information is increasing each year thus enabling future action and costs to be studied.

- Protection of the physical condition of the information and the cover it is stored in.

- The best format for the information to be stored in (both financially and for ease of access).

- Where it is to be stored (on or off site, centrally, decentralized or satellite areas).

- What type of storage is the most efficient (linear cupboards, hanging files, mobile shelving, film, electronic, etc.).

- What tracking systems, if any, would benefit both the information and access to it (bar codes, radio identification tags, electronic software, paper registers, etc.)

The following should also be considered.

- Reducing duplication of retention standards by unifying guidance in one corporate document.

- Reviewing retention and disposal guidance, with reference to national guidance including the Records Management Society's Local Authority Retention and Disposal Guidelines and current legislation.

- Checking of high-level business functions to ensure that all are included in the retention guidance.

- Producing a programme of work for the introduction of the retention schedule.

- How to raise awareness of retention and disposal among employees.

Benefits for disaster management

Implementing these recommendations means that the organization will be in a better state to prepare a contingency plan or records management disaster control plan in order to continue business should a disaster of some type happen. Statistics suggest that 80 per cent of private businesses that suffer such disasters go out of business within two years. According to the Department for Communities and Local Government, the cost as a consequence of fire including property damage, human casualties and lost business was estimated at £2.5 billion for 2004. (There were over 33,400 fires in non-domestic buildings in the same period.) For local authorities it can cause huge embarrassment and cost. You can prevent this from happening by thinking about such events now. What are your most valuable pieces of information? How can you protect them? Will you be able to get to the information in the event of a disaster? Would the information to pay your staff be available? Will they continue to work if they are not being paid? Talk to the experts such as the local fire brigade and your insurance company for free advice. There are also several companies specializing in the recovery of information that has been subjected to fire, explosion, water or insect damage.

Chapter 5 – The retention schedule

The retention schedule gives evidential weight to information through a good regular business practice – i.e. it is an authorized part of the daily business routine as opposed to being carried out on an ad-hoc basis. When defending an action in court, the fact that authorized actions have been carried out on a regular basis will carry more weight.

A retention and disposal schedule should:

- show correct functions, activities, titles and colloquial names of records;
- define a time for retention from a specific time or trip reason (i.e. the trigger for retention);
- show the authority for this decision;
- quote details of the appropriate Act, regulation, circular, code of practice or business practice;
- define who is responsible for the information (the organization owns it but someone must be responsible for it);
- list all known record series regardless of format (i.e. paper, film or electronic);
- identify vital/prime information as opposed to management information (this reminds employees which information should be protected or backed up).

It may also show:

- the general security level of a file series;
- which file series are affected by the Data Protection Act 1998;
- information that may be exempt under the Freedom of Information Act 2000;

- information falling under the Environmental Information Regulations 2004.

The retention schedule should treat all similar information in the same way regardless of the format in which it is received or stored. It does not matter whether the information is received by email, on a CD, stored on a microform or is 'hard' information such as rock samples – the set or recommended period of retention is for the information *not* the storage format. (See Appendix H for detailed advice on email and electronic formats.)

Classification

When it is known what information is held, it can be classified or grouped by activity, function, department, etc. to assist in easy retrieval and efficient organization. The result should be workable within the organization. One of the most common methods of classification is by function since this is least likely to change, whereas activities and departments tend to merge and divide.

Some organizations document this with a map of the hierarchies to find out which sections are responsible for the information and those that share or swap information.

A range of subjects that are being used in the public sector can be viewed under the Integrated Public Sector Vocabulary http://www.esd.org.uk/standards/ipsv/ipsv.doc.

Possible functions or activities of a local authority

1 Cemeteries and crematoria

2 Consumer and animal protection (includes licensing and registers)

3 Corporate management (includes project management)

4 Council land and premises

5 Crime

6 Customer services

7 Democracy or democratic services

8 Economic development

9 Education and learning

---

10 Emergency services

11 Environmental protection

12 Finance

13 Health and safety

14 Housing

15 Human resources

16 Information and communication technology (ICT)

17 Information management (includes data protection and freedom of information)

18 Legal services (includes land charges)

19 Leisure and culture (includes parks)

20 Planning and building control

21 Plant, equipment and stores

22 Public relations

23 Registration (births, deaths and marriages) and coroners

24 Risk management and insurance

25 Social care (adults and children)

26 Transport and highways

27 Waste management

Possible functions or activities of a private organization

1 Corporate management

2 Customer services

3 Environmental issues

4 Facilities management (land, buildings, furniture, etc.)

5 Finance (or accounting)

6 Health and safety

7   Human resources

8   Information and communication technology

9   Information management (includes data protection and in some cases freedom of information)

10 Legal services

11 Public relations (includes advertising)

12 Risk management and insurance

13 Sales

14 Transport

Contents of the retention schedule

A number of pieces of information need to be assembled in order to complete a retention and disposal schedule. These are defined in the following sections. Some will be mandatory, while others will be optional.

Function (mandatory)

This will be a main heading under which a particular type of information will appear. (See examples above for possible headings.)

Record/information type (mandatory)

This defines the record (information type) to which this entry relates. As an example, the record type of 'sales invoices' could be used to identify one of the types of output from your invoicing system. Such a definition is specific and identifies only one type of record.

Alternatively, in some applications it is possible to use a broader definition for the record type. For example, it may be appropriate to identify 'accounting records' in general as a document type. All general correspondence could be placed under one heading regardless of department.

When deciding upon names for record types, it should be clear what is meant by the designation used. In some instances, a description will be needed. So, to many people, a record type of 'BI 510' will be meaningless without a note that BI 510 is also known as the 'accident book'. Conversely, titles such as the 'green book' or 'C & D book' may mean nothing to others without the official title of Collection and Deposit. Look at the entries as if you are a researcher in 50 years' time trying to find out how your organization functioned and why.

Another issue to be avoided is repetition of title. Where schedules are broken down into departments, each showing personnel files and health and safety files, there may be repetition of retention information. Where this occurs, review its appropriateness when compared to having a retention schedule where each file series or type of information is shown only once. Where there is a retention schedule per department then the risk of different retention times for the same information becomes high, especially as time goes by.

When listing types of information, those that are produced for internal purposes should not be forgotten. Information such as procedures, technology descriptions, policies and audit information should also be included within the retention schedule. Information marked 'personal' should be just that – personal to the employee. This sort of information is not included in the schedule but everything else needs to be considered.

There are advantages in using generic titles in the retention schedule. They avoid the need to revamp the schedule every time there are changes in departmental or section titles. They also reduce or eliminate the need to decide in which department to list a particular document type, especially when it could sit under any one of a number of departments (e.g. legal, health and safety, or employee records). Where there is a need to specify specific departments, and there is a conflict, the decision should be based on the most important content; and cross-referenced in the other department records.

Examples of generic titles or functions

- Financial information

- Health and safety information

- Human resources

- Legal information

These can then be broken down into more detailed headings, for easy reference.

For example:

Human Resources

1 Disability

2 Disciplinary action

3 Employment law

4 Equal opportunities

5 Jobs/posts

6 Leave

7 Pay

8 Personnel information (excluding health and safety)

9 Policies and procedures

10 Recruitment

11 Sickness information

12 Trade union matters

13 Training information

14 Youth training

15 Working time

Retention period (mandatory)

The retention period defines the period of time for which the record will need to be kept. This will be as stated in legislation, codes of practice, business regulations or set by the organization itself. If the latter, it should state that the period is recommended and, if possible, reasons given in the 'Notes' column. The retention period is usually a number of months or years from the date of creation, or from the end of the relevant time period. Sometimes the period will date from the closure of a file in which the records are stored. On other occasions, the period may depend on some external event, such as the completion of litigation where the record is evidence in support of this. These are known as trigger actions.

Accounting records, for example, may have a retention period of the current year plus 6 years or 12 years after the completion of the contract.

Information may be:

- current – generally in day-to-day or week-to-week use;

- semi-current – the information has been used for the initial work and subsequent use is minimal;

- reviewable – the information has not been used for some time but has a date allocated to it to check whether it can be destroyed or sent to the archive. (Beware – some people keep putting review dates on information in order to save themselves having to make a decision on its future);

- permanent – a decision has been made to retain the information for research purposes after the business use has been completed.

Determining retention periods

The retention period chosen for a particular record type will depend on a number of factors, including:

- minimum legal requirements – although these can be accessed on websites and through various publications, the only official source is the published article sold through The Stationery Office Ltd (TSO);

- regulatory requirements;

- code of practice recommendations;

- organizational requirements;

- good working practices;

- common practices.

Depending upon your industry sector, you may be working under some rules defined and audited by regulators (for example, in the financial sector there is the Financial Services Authority). These organizations need to be contacted to find out what rules they impose on the retention of records. Good advice on retention is often given on the regulator's website.

Both legal and regulatory requirements will specify minimum time periods that must be adhered to. There may be a justification for internal purposes for keeping records for longer than these minimum periods. There are no general rules to this, as they depend upon the organization's policies and need for historical records. It is up to each organization to determine any additional retention period that it wishes to implement. This should be based on a business risk assessment:

$$\frac{\text{benefits of destruction}}{\text{research value}} \quad \times \quad \frac{\text{storage costs}}{\text{embarrassment of not being able to produce the information}}$$

Such decisions should be documented to show their justification.

If the records contain personal data, then the Data Protection Act 1998 is applicable. Here, there is a requirement to destroy information (confidentially) once the purpose for which it was acquired has been completed. Principle 5 of the Act states that information is to be kept no longer than is necessary. *It is up to the organization to determine when this is* – clearly showing the need for a retention and disposal schedule.

Once a retention period has been defined it is important that the definition chosen is clearly understood. In particular, it should be easy to identify when the retention period starts.

Example of a retention period

An example of a retention period relates to an organization's accident book. Here, defined in the Social Security Act 1992, section 8, is the requirement to keep the record for a period of *three years after the date of the last entry*. For a small organization that has few accidents, this may be a very long time, as the accident book will never be filled up! However, for organizations that keep their accident book on a computer, where the concept of a 'full book' does not exist, there is a greater risk of losing the information or keeping it for longer than necessary. (Principle 5 of the DPA.)

The above example is one in which the retention period is not a fixed time period, but depends upon the occurrence of a specific event.

As another example, a financial organization offering mortgages may decide to keep original application forms for as long as the mortgage is open, plus a fixed time period after closure. Such retention periods are increasingly being used by organizations as an easier to manage system. The Limitation Act 1980 and Prescription and Limitation (Scotland) Act 1973 may have a bearing, especially on land, tort and compensation matters.

Mixed retention periods

Some files may have several types of information requiring differing retention periods. The choice here is to 'weed out' information when necessary or leave all the information in the file until the latest date. This should be the subject of a business risk assessment based on storage capacity, legislation, regulatory requirements and resources available. Personnel files may fall in this category if they contain leave forms, sickness history, pension history, etc. Some of this information may be disposed of on a yearly basis; other types (like the pension information) may need to be kept for a fixed period (for example, 6 or 12 years after the last pension payment).

Indefinite retention

A frequent trap that many fall into is to use a retention period of indefinite length. What does this mean in practice? As an example, when reviewing the retention schedule for a school, one entry read 'School Log Books – indefinitely'. It is unlikely that such a requirement is reasonable. In current practice the probability is the school will keep them for the current year plus six more and pass them on to the archivist or local history officer where appropriate.

A retention period of indefinite length often indicates that no decision has been taken on how long the record needs to be kept. If there is a requirement not to destroy particular records (perhaps because they are of historical interest), it is better to specify an appropriate retention period, and then note that the record should be transferred to an archive for long-term storage.

The Financial Services Authority and some Scottish legislation have examples of a requirement to retain certain information indefinitely. This means the paper forms or electronic information must still be available and readable even after a period of 1000 years!

Example

Scottish Statutory Instrument 2004 No. 428, Building Procedures Section 57(3) Part 1 of the Building Standards Register shall be maintained by the local authority for all time

---

It is not clear from the Scottish legislation example what the word 'maintain' means. Does it mean every piece of information in the register must be retained indefinitely or does it mean the local authority has some discretion over when certain information may be removed as long as the register remains in existence? (This would be like maintaining an old car to keep it running.) Reading the legislation it seems to indicate that all information should be retained.

For information that seems to fall under no other legislation, the Limitation Act 1980 and the Prescription and Limitation (Scotland) Act 1973 are often quoted.

A synopsis of these two pieces of legislation is shown in Appendices D and E respectively. The details shown are for guidance and organizations wishing to use the legislation should consult their legal representatives for full legal interpretations.

Media type (optional)

With the increasing use of computer systems to store electronic records, it is important to specify in the retention schedule how a record will be stored. If such a column is used it can indicate what is specified in the legislation – i.e. 'To be in writing' or it can show how long it is stored in one medium before being transferred to another – e.g. '12 months' paper then microfilmed'. Thus if information on paper is microfilmed after 12 months and the paper destroyed, it saves a searcher looking for a format that does not exist.

Storage media can be classified into several formats.

Paper

This is the traditional media type for storage. Many records arrive in an organization, or are created within the organization, in paper form and are kept in this form for the whole of their retention period. Where information is kept in paper form, it should be stored in folders with covers that show relevant details from the records retention and disposal schedule, or at least references to relevant documentation. Such sheets could be printed on 'Crack-Back Plus'™ for ease of application See Appendix B for an example. The information required on the covers of the paper format should match similar information retained in other formats such as 'folders' on a PC. It may also be appropriate to include some information about the organization's records management policy and procedures within each file. This information could be on a 'top sheet' (i.e. all information is filed behind it).

Electronic storage – non-rewritable

Non-rewritable storage has a physical characteristic of information being unable to be altered once it has been written. Examples of media that have this characteristic are microfilm (in many different formats and layouts) and specific types of optical disk (designated WORM media). Other non-rewritable forms are also becoming available as technology progresses.

Electronic storage – rewritable

Typical examples of rewritable electronic storage are computer hard disks (local or networked), magnetic tape and some forms of optical disk. With this type of media, it is technically possible, given the right system access, to erase and amend existing records.

Mixed media

It may be appropriate for some information within an organization to be 'migrated' from one media type to another during its retention period. For example, information may be received in paper form, and scanned to produce an electronic copy in image form. An appropriate retention schedule entry might then be to retain the original paper record for three months, but to retain the electronic version for seven years. There are cases where permission has been given for income tax or VAT records to be scanned or filmed to assist ease of access and retained for the current year plus six years but the paper record can be disposed of after three years. (The need to keep it for three years is to give time to check original signatures if necessary.) This is usually where the organization is following recommended standards. Those organizations that have no proper policy or are unable or unwilling to comply with acceptable records management standards are usually required to keep the paper copies for the full term.

Hard media

Rock or drill samples and specimens for court cases are examples of hard media.

Example of hard media

One example is the keeping of a banana skin that a member of the public claimed to have slipped on while on the organization's premises. This was stored in an airtight plastic bag with a retention period covering completion of the court case plus six years in case of any appeals or further claims of damage. Whether the evidence would be in a suitable state by that time is another matter!

Storage location (optional)

It is an important function of a records retention schedule to ensure that information can be retrieved when it is needed for a business purpose such as a subject access request under the Data Protection Act 1998 or the Freedom of Information Act 2000. Thus, a 'where it is stored' or 'current location' field may be required.

Responsibilities (optional)

The records management policy must specify who can create or amend the schedule information and who has the authority to take disposal action at the end of the retention period. This should be expressed in the form of job titles rather than individuals' names, to avoid the need for updating after changes of personnel. This information could also be made available in the schedule either on a separate sheet at the front or in a note at the start of each function or even by an entry on each line.

Typical responsibilities include the following.

- Creation – what is allowed into the system and when?

- Storage – in what format should the information be stored?

- Disposition – what is to happen to the information at the end of its business life? Should it be retained for research or destroyed? If destroyed, by what means? If placed into archives, are there to be any restrictions such as time before viewing is allowed or available to a certain type of researcher?

- Amendments – who is allowed to amend the specified retention period? It is for each organization to allocate this responsibility. It may be one or more persons but the more persons granted this action the more likely duplication or errors will appear.

Disposition (mandatory)

The records retention schedule should identify what needs to be done to each information type, at the end of its retention period as business information. Not all information will be disposed of in the same way. There may be a requirement for confidential disposal (to varying levels of security), or the need for selective identification of information for long-term preservation in an archive. Again, this could be on a separate sheet at the beginning of the schedule.

Authority (mandatory)

To fulfil its potential, the schedule should be presented to the appropriate authority within the organization (usually the board) for approval. Part of the approval process may include reviews and approval by legal, regulatory and audit groups to ensure compliance with the organization's obligations to keep complete records of its operations. This authority could be shown at the start of the schedule.

Specimen retention schedule

The retention and disposal schedule should contain guidelines on its content and use. A typical information sheet has been reproduced in Appendix C as a guide to what could be included on this page.

Page 36 shows a typical page from a retention schedule.

Ref No

The first heading (Ref No) refers to the main and subsection reference numbers, following a numerical sequence. Experience has shown this simplifies finding a particular information series, especially when needing rapid access to a particular type of information.

Title of Document [Local name]

Information often has two names – the official name and the colloquial name. It is best to show both with the colloquial name in square brackets, e.g. BI 510 [Accident Book]. There may be a need for a separate column, or an indicator in this column, to indicate if the file series is affected by the Data Protection Act 1998 or the Freedom of Information Act 2000.

Retention Period

The retention period should, wherever possible, be specific and state a trigger event such as a particular date, time period, event, etc.

Current Format

This is to be used as a guide so that persons looking for information know what format (e.g. media type) to look for, and so that in the case of e.g. 'three years paper/four years microfilm' they know not to look for the paper format after the third year, especially if your organization destroys paper records after filming. Alternatively, it may show what the legislation specifies, i.e. whether the record is to be in writing, may be kept electronically or kept in any media that can be read by the human eye.

Authority

This column shows the authority on which the retention decision was made. 'Corporate' or 'Audit' is the organization's decision, which in some cases may exceed the statutory requirement. Where the word 'Statutory' appears, the full name of the Act or Statutory Instrument together with the relevant section or regulation should be quoted in the Notes/Access column. This should avoid argument but, if not, the legislation can easily be referred to. 'Statutory' also covers approved codes of practice.

Notes/Access

This gives details of the statutes and codes of practice where indicated under 'Authority'. It may also indicate actions such as:

- destroy by shredding;

- pass to archives;

- consult local history officer.

(Some organizations may prefer a separate column for these actions.)

This column must be regularly reviewed to ensure the information is up to date but beware – new legislation does not always revoke previous legislation in its entirety. The information-keeping aspect is not always retrospective and therefore the previous statute may still cover earlier information. This column may also indicate who is responsible for the information. Alternatively, the responsibility could appear under the name of the document or information.

P/M

This denotes prime or management information (prime information is information that if lost would cause considerable financial loss or embarrassment). 'Prime' is chosen as opposed to the usual 'vital' because employees usually believe all their information to be 'vital'. However, there appears to be no such problem with the use of 'prime'. Information not classified as prime is designated as 'management information' and is not vital to the running of the organization or can easily be replaced or reconstituted.

Security

A further column may be added that shows the general level of security for the file series. If this is done it must be remembered that it is 'general' and that any single piece of information within the series may, at some time, be classified at a different level. The levels and terminology used for this will have to be set by the organization.

Table 1 — Example of a retention schedule layout. Specimen only – not to be used as a working copy

Section 4 Health and Safety Records

Ref No	Title of Document [Local Name]	Retention Period	Current Format	Authority	Notes/Access	P/M
4.1	**Accident Records**					
4.1.1	Accident forms/ reports	Current Year + 6 years	Paper/electronic	Corporate	Includes associated papers	P
4.1.2	BI 510 [Accident books]	3 years after last entry	To be in writing. (May be in paper or electronic format)	Statutory	Social Security (Claims and Payments) Regulations 1979, Regulation 25. Social Security Administration Act 1992, section 8.	P
4.1.3	RIDDOR F2508 F2508A	3 years from date of notification	Paper/microfilm	Statutory	Reporting of Injuries, Diseases and Dangerous Occurrences Regulations 1995, Regulation 7: Records	M
4.1.4	Off-site emergency plan	For duration of the activity with updating for significant changes	To be in writing including email or by such other means as the recipient may allow	Statutory	The Control of Major Accident Hazards Regulations 1999 SI 1999 No 743, Regulation 9 (1)	P

Chapter 6 – Implementing and managing the retention schedule

So now you have a draft retention and disposal schedule. Who is going to approve it? This differs between organizations. It could be the chief executive, the board, company secretary, head of legal, head of audit or a council meeting. What is important is that it is approved at a high level within the organization so that it carries weight both with employees and in law should the organization face litigation.

Once approved the retention schedule should be circulated or made available to all staff either in paper or electronic form. It is of little value to an organization to produce a retention schedule and then place it on a shelf – never to be used.

It is an advantage if it is available via an intranet and better still if it is incorporated into an EDRMS (electronic document records management system) to enable the allocation of an automatic retention period together with a reminder when the information is to be disposed of as business information.

Such a system can automate or assist workflow, classification, searching and disposition. It will provide audit trails, including proof of destruction. Such a system also stores the metadata (i.e. data about data – context, content and structure) about the information.

Making the schedule available does not always mean employees will use or understand it, so there may be the need for workshops to explain to managers or other employees how and why they need to understand and use the system.

Should a retention schedule be managed at department or section level, or corporately? If individual managers are allowed to make amendments then things soon become messy, with different managers applying different periods of retention. If managed centrally then the schedule is easier to update and keep consistent. It also means everybody receives the same information at the same time, especially if held on, or distributed by the intranet. If an intranet version is amended then it is worth placing a notification of change on the system, as many people rely on memory to carry out actions.

Even if managed at a corporate level by the records manager then any additions, amendments or deletions will still require the approval of the board, audit or whoever authorized the original document according to the directions in the records management policy. All such changes should be documented to provide an audit trail.

Chapter 7 – Disposition – destruction and archive

> Average rental cost of space in central London is £500 per square metre per year. A medium-sized filing room could cost as much as £25,000 per year.
>
> Valuation Office Agency. Page 40 M-iD November 2005.

Disposition – moving the information on

When information is no longer of day-to-day use in the business it should be moved on – either to another storage format to reduce space, to off-site storage, to the archives or destroyed.

Methods of destruction will depend on the format and the sensitivity. Information might be thrown in a bin or it might need to be hogged, shredded, pulped or burnt. Whatever steps are taken for destruction ensure that all back-up copies and duplicates are also destroyed or else your organization will still be 'holding the information' and will need to produce it if required in law. This could be both embarrassing and costly.

In cases of investigation by police or audit, all destruction procedures on the information concerned must cease immediately.

Non-confidential information can be thrown into the usual paper bins but it is better if it can be recycled and many organizations encourage this.

If the information is sensitive then it can be hogged, shredded or burnt.

Shredding means cutting into strips and, if the information is sensitive, cross-cutting it to make it smaller and harder to piece together. The result can then be recycled. It can also be shredded and burnt or simply burnt.

However, this can be expensive and a waste of resources and therefore should only be used where really necessary. There are shredders that will reduce information to dust, but they tend to be big and noisy. Even film, tape and floppies can be put through shredders designed for them.

'Hogging' is where paper is machine-ripped into pieces of various sizes. The results are then wired together in one-tonne bales and re-pulped and recycled.

All but non-sensitive information needs to be held in locked rooms or containers while awaiting disposal through a system that leaves an audit trail. It is not much use to say two tonnes of paper were destroyed on 12 May 2006. You should have a certificate for what information was destroyed, by whom, when and by what method. This certificate should be filed with the authority to destroy. Without such a certificate you will not be able to prove beyond all reasonable doubt that it has been destroyed rather than lost or misfiled. If you have a BS EN ISO 9000 system, this should be part of it.

For hard drives you should consult your IT department on the most thorough but cost-effective method of completely destroying the information. Remember, systems can be restored to a previous state using software that is part of the computer's own operating system. Commercial un-delete or recovery software is also available.

When destroying information in accordance with the retention schedule, include all back-ups and copies. Failure to do so may mean you are still 'holding information' that may have to be produced in court or at a tribunal. (See Information Tribunal Appeal number EA/2005/0001. An extract is shown in Appendix G.)

In the end the method of destruction comes down to a business risk assessment – i.e. the cost of destruction versus the embarrassment or financial loss caused if the information were to get into the hands of the press, a member of the public or a competitor.

Care needs to be taken over the destruction of information. The following should be considered.

- Can you afford the internal resource to carry out the destruction or is it cheaper to contract it out?

- Will your agency cleaners have access to information for disposal?

- Which staff should handle information for destruction?

- Do you need locked holding bins or a secure room?

- Should you shred the paper before handing it over for recycling?

- Will the contractor let you make spot checks on their premises?

- Will the information be transported in a locked vehicle?

- Will the vehicle have wire mesh sides through which whole sheets could be read when the vehicle is stopped?

- If the contractor destroys information on your site do you need to allocate a member of staff to ensure that it is securely carried out?

- Will the information be stored in the open or in an open-sided barn before destruction?

- Will the information be stored and destroyed under cover where the wind cannot blow it away?

- What sort of security does the destruction site have?

- Is any sort of check made on the contractor's employees to ensure they are trustworthy? (Principle 7 of the DPA.)

Chapter 8 – Summary

Before you can formulate a retention and disposal schedule you need to know what you hold. This may be achieved by an 'information audit' preferably authorized at the highest level. The results of the audit should be divided into a workable 'classification scheme' that reflects the organization's business needs.

From this information a 'retention and disposal schedule' can be formed detailing what types of information are held, how long to hold them for and in what format. This will include any legislative or business practices for the time scale.

Armed with the retention and disposal schedule, the organization can then safely remove all information that is no longer relevant or required, thus freeing up valuable space while knowing that it should be safe from litigation.

Having identified its information assets and made the appropriate safeguards for the vital information the organization has started the process of business continuity and may wish to continue the process by following the processes laid out in BS 25999-1, *Code of practice for business continuity management.*

Appendix A – Information survey form (specimen)

1. Directorate/Group	2. Building/floor	3. Section/Team Manager Day-to-day responsibility
4. What is the information series called?	5. Purpose of information	6. Telephone/ext./email

| 7. What is the format? ✓ as appropriate

Paper ☐   Film ☐
Electronic ☐   Hard ☐
If electronic ✓ format
CD ☐   Tape ☐
Floppy ☐   Hard drive ☐
Server ☐   Other ☐ | 8. Which other Sections/Teams have access to them?

9. Finding aids | 10. How many individual records in the series?

10a. If paper or film – type of storage

10b. Linear metreage/cms/ megabytes

10c. Annual growth |

11. How often are they accessed? ✓	12. How long do you need to keep this information? ✓	
Less than once a month? ☐	Less than 1 year ☐	Less than 2 years ☐
At least once a month but not every week? ☐	2 to 6 years ☐	6 to 10 years ☐
	10 to 25 years ☐	25 to 50 years ☐
At least once a week but not every day? ☐	50 to 100 years ☐	Archived for research ☐
Daily? ☐		

13. State the reason for the retention period	14. Does a duplicate exist? ✓
	Yes ❑ No ❑ Don't know ❑
	If yes where?
	In what form?
	Paper ❑ Film ❑ Electronic ❑
	If electronic what format?
	CD ❑ Tape ❑ Floppy ❑
	Hard drive ❑ Server ❑ Other ❑

15. The loss of certain information through fire or some other disaster would have very serious consequences for the organization's operations. Does this information fall into this category? ✓

Yes ❑   No ❑   Do not know ❑

If yes please explain why.

16. Is this information subject to FOI/DPA legislation?

FOI   Release ❑   Exempt ❑   Why?

DPA   Release ❑   Exempt ❑   Why?

17. Any other comments

Form completed by

Date

Notes for completing the questionnaire

1. *Directorate/Group*

The part of the organization directly responsible for the information and its use.

2. *Building/Floor*

The location of the person responsible for the information.

3. *Section/Team Manager/Day-to-day responsibility*

The name of the head of the section or team, or alternatively the day-to-day user of the information.

4. *What is the information series called?*

There is usually a formal title and a colloquial title, e.g. BI 510, which is usually known as the accident book.

5. *Purpose of information*

What the information is used for within the organization.

6. *Telephone/ext./email*

The contact details of the user.

7. *What is the format?*

- Paper – e.g. A4, A3, maps, books, folders, etc.
- Film – e.g. microfilm, analogue CCTV
- Electronic – e.g. CD, tape, floppy disk, hard drive, server or other (flash drives, etc.)
- Hard – e.g. rock samples, items to be used as court evidence.

This enables an informed decision to be made about the way forward concerning possible standardization, compatibility and migration.

8. *Which other Sections/Teams have access to them?*

This section shows shared information. Can the information be shared more easily and controlled if put in another format? (It is possible to share information without additional copies, however, note question 14.)

9. *Finding aids*

How do the users find the information, e.g. by:

- account number;

- address;
- card index;
- electronic index;
- name of person or organization;
- serial number;
- some other method.

10. *How many individual records in the series?*

The number of file covers or equivalent electronic records in the series.

This information, when taken with the type and amount of storage plus the annual growth and frequency of access, allows an informed decision to be taken regarding the future of the information.

10a. *If paper or film – type of storage*

For example, cupboard, filing cabinet, open shelf, floor, desk, hanging files, fire safe, data safe, etc.

10b. *Linear metreage/cms/megabytes*

Most users are happy to measure the space occupied in metres or part of a metre. If the storage shelves are all the same length then the number of shelves is acceptable.

The measure of megabytes is usually more difficult for users if they are not familiar with the use of the 'properties' tool on a PC. It is sometimes easier to ask the IT people for a print out of the amount of electronic storage for a particular type of information.

10c. *Annual growth*

An indication of whether existing storage will be sufficient to cope or whether it needs to be increased or a different format put in place to reduce space needed, ensuring of course that access is just as easy or easier.

11. *How often are they accessed?*

This information can give guidance on possible future formats and storage possibilities making it easier to access or to free up space for other information.

12. *How long do you need to keep this information?*

Initially this is the view of the user of the information. It frequently changes during probing questions from the auditor.

13. *State the reason for the retention period*

Be prepared for some unusual answers! 'It shows the sort of work I have been doing since I joined the organization' has been one reply. The ideal answer would be one quoting the relevant legislation, guidance or code of practice.

14. *Does a duplicate exist?*

It is usual for many duplicates to exist especially with information such as meeting minutes. The auditor needs to know if there are duplicates, who holds them and, more importantly, which is the master or legal copy. (See question 8 – it is possible to share without there being a duplicate.)

15. *The loss of certain information through fire or some other disaster would have very serious consequences for the organization's operations. Does this information fall into this category?*

This is the view of the user of the information together with their reasons for making the decision. If the view is accepted then the information will need to have a back-up policy to protect it from loss or damage.

16. *Is this information subject to the Freedom of Information Act 2000 or Data Protection Act 1998?*

This is initially for the user to complete. The answer given should be discussed with the Freedom of Information and Data Protection Officer. Investigation may show the user to be wrong in their assessment.

17. *Any other comments*

This is for completion both by the user of the information and the auditor for any thing not covered above. For example, it may carry a comment such as 'the information held is always 6 months old when received'.

Appendix B – Specimen file cover

File Number	(London Borough of Nonsuch)	Security Classification	
Part	(Any Organization plc)		
Title/Subject		Opened	Closed
Group	Section	Officer	Prime document ☐
			Management document ☐
To	Date	To	Date	To	Date	To	Date
---	---	---	---	---	---	---	---

Retention action

Access action

Archival action

Appendix C – Specimen guidance sheet

RETENTION and DISPOSAL OF DOCUMENTS SCHEDULE

This schedule has been updated according to Acts of Parliament, Statutory Instruments and current business practices. It carries the authorization of [insert as appropriate: internal audit/the auditors/the organization's solicitors, etc.].

Any additions, deletions or amendments should be forwarded to [name of responsible authority].

The information will be used by the Main Registry to ensure records are properly maintained.

The retention period specified applies whatever the format – paper, microfilm or electronic.

Disposal at the end of the retention period should be as follows:

- paper – via the confidential waste paper system;
- microforms – via the Main Registry for shredding;
- electronic – by deletion from the hard/floppy disk or by sending the floppy to the Main Registry for shredding.

Notes

Title of Document   Should be the official name. Colloquial names should appear in square brackets. [ ]

\#   Indicates the contents may be affected by the Data Protection Act 1998.

$ Indicates the contents may be affected by the Freedom of Information Act 2000.

CY	Current year.
Current Format	Gives guidance on the current storage format.
Corporate/Audit	Indicates the organization's decision. It may be in excess of the legal time scale.
P/M	Indicates prime or management documentation. (Some organizations use vital and management.) Prime documents must always be backed up and retained for statutory or audit reasons.
	A prime document is one that if lost would cause considerable public, legal or financial embarrassment to the organization.
	Duplicates are **not** prime documents. Management documents should generally be kept for the current year plus two.
To be in writing	Under more recent legislation this may also include electronic communication – as defined in the Electronic Communications Act 2003 – that has been recorded and is consequently capable of being reproduced.

In cases of investigation by police or audit all destruction procedures on the information concerned must cease immediately.

Appendix D – Limitation Act 1980 (excludes Scotland) – periods of action

NOTE: This is a synopsis of the Act for guidance only. Organizations are strongly advised to seek clarification from their legal advisers before acting on the contents.

Subject	Recommended retention period	Section of the Act
Tort	6 years after action.	Section 2
Recovery of goods	6 years.	
Defamation	1 year from date of action.	
Libel		
Slander		
Malicious falsehood		
Slander of title		
Slander of goods		
Simple contract	6 years from end date.	Section 5
Not under seal	6 years from end date.	
Speciality	12 years from end date.	
Sums recoverable by statute	6 years.	See also section 10, claiming contribution.

Subject	Recommended retention period	Section of the Act
Claiming contribution	2 years from when right accrued. (Date of award as agreed personally or by court.)	Civil Liability (Contribution Act) 1978.
Personal injuries Negligence Nuisance Breach of duty	3 years from date of cause of action accrued OR Date of knowledge (if later) of the person injured. If person dies then 3 years from date of death or from date of personal representative's knowledge.	Does not apply to actions brought under section 3 of the Protection from Harassment Act 1997.
Defective products	10 years after the relevant time in accordance with section 4 of the Consumer Protection Act 1987.	For personal injuries or loss of property from defective products then 3 years from date of action accrued or date of knowledge.

Subject	Recommended retention period	Section of the Act
Actions under Fatal Accidents Act 1976	3 years from date of death or date of knowledge of the person for whose benefit the action is brought – whichever is the later.	Date of knowledge is the date of the following facts: 1. that the injury was significant; 2. or was attributable in whole or part to the act of omission constituting negligence, nuisance or breach of duty; 3. the identity of the defendant is known; 4. the act or omission was a person other than the defendant.
Negligence where relevant facts are not known at date of accrual	6 years from date on which the cause of action accrued or 3 years from the starting date of knowledge.	
Negligence not involving personal injuries	11 years from date of act or omission.	Latent Damage Act 1986.

Subject	Recommended retention period	Section of the Act
Action to recover land	12 years from the date on which the right of action occurred OR 6 years from the date on which the right of action accrued to the person entitled to the succeeding estate or interest. Whichever period last expires.	
Redemption actions	12 years.	
Settled land and land held on trust	12 years.	Settled Land Act 1925.
Rent recovery	6 years from when it becomes due.	
Recovery of money secured by mortgage or charge or to recover proceeds of the sale of land	12 years from the date on which the right to receive the money accrued.	No foreclosure action in respect of mortgaged property shall be brought after the expiration of 12 years from the date on which the right to foreclose accrued.

Subject	Recommended retention period	Section of the Act
Arrears of interest on mortgage, other charge or payable in respect of proceeds of the sale of land or to recover damages in respect of such arrears	6 years from date on which interest became due.	
Trust property	No limit in respect of fraud or fraudulent breach of trust; otherwise 6 years.	
Claiming personal estate of a deceased person	12 years for claims relating to the personal estate or interest in any such estate. 6 years in respect of any legacy or damages in respect of such arrears.	
Actions to enforce judgements	6 years from when the judgement became enforceable. Interest on judgement of debt – 6 years from date interest became due.	

Subject	Recommended retention period	Section of the Act
Cure of defective disentailing assurance	12 years from when the assurance could have operated as an effective bar.	
Extension of limitation period in case of disability	6 years from date when the individual ceased to be under the disability or died (whichever is first). 30 years from the right of action accrued in respect of recovery of land or money charged on land. 1 year in the case of action for slander, libel, slander of goods and other malicious falsehoods. 2 years in the case of claiming contributions. 3 years for personal injuries.	

Subject	Recommended retention period	Section of the Act
Modification of section 15 where Crown or certain corporations sole are involved	Recovery of any land by the Crown or eleemosynary corporation sole – 30 years. Action to recover foreshore by the Crown – 60 years. Right of action to recover land that has ceased to be foreshore but remains in Crown ownership: • 60 years from date of accrual of right of action; • 30 years from the date when land ceased to be foreshore; whichever period first expires.	

NOTE:

1. The Act shall not apply to any proceedings by the Crown for the recovery of any tax or duty or interest on any tax or duty.

2. The Act shall not apply to any forfeiture proceedings under the Customs and Excise Acts within the meaning of the Custom and Excise Management Act 1979.

3. The Act shall not apply to any proceedings in respect of the forfeiture of a ship.

4. The Act shall not apply if a period of limitation is prescribed by or under any other Act whether passed before or after the passing of this Act.

5. The Act does not extend to Scotland or Northern Ireland.

Interpretation

'Action' includes any proceedings in a court of law, including ecclesiastical courts.

'Land' includes corporate hereditaments, tithes rent charges and any legal or equitable estate or interest therein. But does not necessarily include incorporeal hereditament.

'Personal estate' and 'personal property' do not include chattels real.

'Personal injuries' includes any disease and any impairment of a person's physical or mental condition and 'injury' and cognate expressions shall be construed accordingly.

'Rent' includes a rent charge and a rent service. Rent charge means any annuity or periodical sum of money charged upon or payable out of land except a rent service or interests on a mortgage of land.

'Settled land', 'statutory owner' and 'tenant for life' have the same meanings respectively as in the Settled Land Act 1925.

'Trust' and 'trustee' have the same meanings respectively as in the Trustee Act 1925.

'Under a disability' for the purpose of this Act is a person who is an infant or of unsound mind (as interpreted by the Mental Health Act 1959, Mental Health Act 1983, Nursing Homes Act 1973 and Care Standards Act 2000).

Appendix E – Prescription and Limitation (Scotland) Act 1973 (replaces the Prescription Acts of 1469, 1474 and 1617)

NOTE: This is a synopsis of the Act for guidance only. Organizations are strongly advised to seek clarification from their legal advisers before acting on the contents.

Periods of action

Land

Positive prescription – Interests in land: General (section 1)

10 years   If the interest has been possessed by any persons and/or by his successors for a continuous period of 10 years without judicial interruption and such possession was founded on and recorded by deed then exempt from challenge except if deed is invalid or was forged.

20 years   If a foreshore or salmon fishing interest then the period is 20 years.

Special cases (lease/allodial land) (section 2)

20 years   If the interest has been possessed by any person and/or successors for a continuous period of 20 years without judicial interruption and such possession was founded on a deed then exempt from challenge except if deed is invalid or was forged.

Positive servitude over land (section 3)

20 years   If servitude possessed for a continuous period of 20 years openly, peaceably and without any judicial interruption and the possession was founded on, and followed, the execution of a deed

which is sufficient in respect of its terms (expressly or by implication) to constitute the servitude then as from the expiration of the said period shall be exempt from challenge on the ground that the deed is invalid *ex facie* or was forged.

Public right of way (section 3)

20 years   If been possessed by the public for a continuous 20 years openly, peaceably and without judicial interruption then as from the expiration of that period of the existence of the right of way it is exempt from challenge.

Extinction of obligations by prescriptive periods

Negative prescription (section 6)

Applies to any obligation to pay a sum of money due in a particular period such as:

- interest;
- instalment of an annuity;
- feu duty or other periodical payment under a feu grant;
- ground annual or other periodical payment under a contract of ground annual;
- rent or other periodical payment under a lease;
- periodical payment in respect of occupancy or use of land not being an obligation falling within any other provision;
- periodical payment under a land obligation not being an obligation falling within any other provision;
- an obligation based on redress of unjustified enrichment;
- obligation arising from *negotiorum gestio*;
- obligation arising from liability to make reparation;
- obligation under bill of exchange or promissory note;
- obligation of accounting other than accounting for trust funds;
- obligation arising from, or by any reason of any breach of, a contract or promise, not being an obligation falling within any other provision of this paragraph.

DOES NOT apply to:

- obligation to recognize or obtemper a decree of court;

- an arbitration award;

- order of a tribunal or authority exercising jurisdiction under any enactment;

- obligation arising from the issue of a bank note;

- obligation constituted or evidenced by a probative writ, not being a cautionary obligation;

- obligation under contract of partnership or of agency not being an obligation remaining or becoming prestable on or after the termination of the relationship between parties under the contract;

- obligation to satisfy any claim to terce, courtesy, legitim, *jus relicti* or *jus relictae* or to any prior right of a surviving spouse under section 8 or 9 of the Succession (Scotland) Act 1964;

- obligation to make reparation in respect of personal injuries within the meaning of Part II of the Act or in respect of death of any persons as a result of injuries;

- any imprescriptible obligations (Schedule 3).

Where by virtue of a probative write co-obligants are bound jointly and severally by an obligation to pay money to another party it shall be regarded as if it were a cautionary obligation unless the concerned co-obligator is truly a principal debtor or if that is not the case that the original creditor was not aware of the fact at the time when the writ was delivered to him.

5 years   If after the appropriate date an obligation has subsisted for a continuous period of 5 years without claim then the obligation is extinguished.

Fraud, induced error or refrain not to count as part of the period.

Obligations to make reparation (section 11) for the purpose of section 6

Any obligation (whether arising from any enactment, or from any rule of law or from, or by reason of any breach of, a contract or promise) to make reparation for loss, injury or damage caused by an act, neglect or default shall be regarded for the purpose of section 6 as becoming enforceable on the date when the loss, injury or damage occurred.

Where as a result of a continuing act, neglect or default loss, injury or damage has occurred before the cessation of the act, neglect or default loss, injury or damage shall be deemed for the purpose to have occurred on the date when the act, neglect or default ceased.

Where the creditor was not aware and could not with reasonable diligence have been aware then the date of the obligation shall be when the creditor first became, or could with reasonable diligence have become, so aware.

In outline:

- with a series of transactions – the time runs from the date on which payment for the goods was last supplied becomes due;

- work or payments by instalments – the time runs from date of last work performed or instalment paid;

- others – from the date when the obligation became enforceable.

Negative prescription (section 7)

20 years   If, after the date when any obligation to which this section applies has become enforceable, the obligation has subsisted for a continuous period of 20 years without any relevant claim having been made in relation to the obligation then as from the expiration of that period the obligation shall be extinguished.

Extinction of other rights relating to property (section 8)

20 years   If, after the date when any right to this section applies has become exercisable or enforceable, the right has subsisted for a continuous period of 20 years unexercised or unenforced and without any relevant claim in relation to it having been made then at the expiration of that period the right shall be extinguished.

Applies to property whether heritable or moveable not being a right specified in Schedule 3 –

Imprescriptible rights and obligations:

- any real right of ownership in land;

- the right in land of the lessee under recorded lease;

- any right exercisable as a res merae facultatis;

- any right to recover property extra commercium;

- any obligation of a trustee:
  - to produce accounts or the trustee's intromissions with any property of the trust;
  - to make reparation or restitution in respect of any fraudulent breach of trust to which the trustee was a party or was privy;
  - to make forthcoming to any person entitled thereto any trust property or the proceeds of any such property or to make good the value of such property previously received by the trustee and appropriated for his own use;
- any obligation of a third party to make forthcoming to any person entitled thereto any trust property received by the third party otherwise than in good faith and in his possession;
- any right to recover stolen property from the person by whom it was stolen or from any person privy to the stealing thereof;
- any right to be served as heir to an ancestor or to take any steps necessary for making up or completing title to any interest in land.

Prohibition of contracting out (section 13)

Any provision in any agreement to contracting out of the obligations of this Act shall be null.

NOTE: Claims under the Consumer Protection Act are subject to the 10 years provision provided by the Act.

Personal injuries

Limitation of actions (section 17)

3 years   No action of damages where the damages consist of, or include, damages or solatium in respect of personal injuries shall be brought against any person unless it is commenced 3 years from the date when the injuries were sustained or where such act, neglect or default was a continuing one then from when it ceased, whichever is the later.

If brought by or on behalf of a person who has died, 3 years from the date of death.

If the person was under a legal disability by reason of nonage, or if on that date the said person was or became under legal disability by reason of unsoundness of mind and in either case that person was not in the custody of a parent the action may be brought at any time within 3 years from the date when that person ceased to be under the disability notwithstanding the period of limitation has expired.

Further extensions are contained in section 19.

- If facts were outside the knowledge of the deceased at all times.

- Where the deceased had brought and immediately before his death was continuing an action.

- Where the facts were outside the knowledge of the person such as a personal representative or executor.

Personal injuries include any disease and any impairment of a person's physical or mental condition (section 22).

Time limit for claiming contribution between wrongdoers (section 20)

2 years   Where, under section 3 of the Law Reform (Miscellaneous Provisions) (Scotland) Act 1940, a person has become or becomes entitled on or after 31 July 1963 to recover damages or expenses then he must do so within 2 years from the date on which that right accrued unless it falls under the legal disability mentioned in section 17 then the period is increased to **3 years**.

This section includes arbitration to recover from a carrier a contribution in respect of damages to which Article 29 in Schedule 1 to the Carriage by Air Act 1961 applies (but check subsequent legislation).

Appendix F – General guidance for retention periods

NOTE: This is not a retention schedule. This guidance should not be relied on in a legal manner until confirmed by a legal source. The legislation quoted is in force at the time of writing but may have been amended or superseded by the time of publication.

Administration

Category	Retention period	Notes
Goods in/out record book	Current plus 6 years	Limitation Act 1980
Stock adjustment sheets	Current year plus 2 years	Audit
Inventories	Until superseded and new inventory has been audited	Commercial practice
Asset registers	Current year plus 6 years	Commercial practice
Contractor time sheets	One year after transfer to accounting systems unless required for VAT/tax purposes	Commercial practice/ Limitation Act 1980
Copy purchase orders	3 years after original sent for payment	Commercial practice
Copy correspondence	3 years after date of correspondence	Commercial practice

Correspondence files	3 to 6 years	Commercial practice
Complaints	3 years unless it results in major changes in policy or working practices; in this case archive	Commercial practice

Corporate documents

Category	Retention period	Notes
Minutes of committee or board meetings (official copy)	The life of the organization	Companies Act 1985
Written resolutions	The life of the organization	Companies Act 1985
Company registers	The life of the organization	Companies Act 1985
Company organization papers (if significant)	The life of the organization	Commercial practice
Significant policy papers	The life of the organization	Commercial practice
Register of seals	The life of the organization	Companies Act 1985
Articles of association or incorporation	The life of the organization	Companies Act 1985
Change of name	The life of the organization	Companies Act 1985
Annual reports	Archive one copy	Commercial practice
Circulars to shareholders	Archive one copy	Commercial practice

Annual meeting proxy and polling cards	Recommend 3 months after meeting if no poll demanded. One year if poll is demanded or meeting convened by court	Commercial practice
Share dealing and administration	12 years after action has ended	Companies Act 1985
Trade and service marks documents	10 years after cessation of registration	Companies Act 1985
Copyright protection	Varies according to type	Copyright, Designs and Patents Act 1988

Human resources

Category	Retention period	Notes
Personnel records (including directors' contracts but excluding pension records)	7 years after employment ceases	Limitation Act 1980
Training course details	6 years after course	Commercial practice
Training course attendees	6 years after course	Commercial practice
Training and continuous personal development records	Add to personnel file	These may be referred to in the case of any litigation concerning neglect or misconduct by either the individual or the organization
Staff appraisals	Current year plus 1 year	Commercial practice

Category	Retention period	Notes
Labour agreements	Until superseded	Commercial practice
Group health/accident policies	12 years after benefit ends	Commercial practice
Patent/secrecy agreements	20 years after employment ceases	Commercial practice
Consolidated sickness records	Current year plus 3 years unless falling under health and safety legislation	Commercial practice/various health and safety legislation
Vacancies and applications (unsuccessful)	6 months	Commercial practice
Early retirement/redundancy documents	6 years after date of retirement	Limitation Act 1980
Secrecy and breach of trust agreements	Length of time stated in agreement	Commercial practice
Disciplinary	Unfounded – destroy immediately Minor – 1 year from date of action Major/final warning – 3 years from date of action	Commercial practice and Data Protection Act 1998
Leave: • adoption • annual • flexi • maternity/paternity • sick • special • time off in lieu	Current year plus 1 year	Commercial practice

Financial records

Accounting records

Category	Retention period	Notes
Cheques	6 years after audit	Limitation Act 1980
Invoices	6 years after audit	Limitation Act 1980
Invoices (capital)	10 years after audit	Commercial practice
Purchase orders	Current year plus 3 years	Audit
Quotations (successful)	Until invoice settled and audited	Audit
Quotations (unsuccessful)	6 months to 1 year	Commercial practice
Customs & Excise returns	Current year plus 6 years	Value Added Tax Act 1994 and Taxes Management Act 1970
VAT deferments	Current year plus 6 years	Value Added Tax Act 1994
Shipping documents	Current year plus 6 years	Limitation Act 1980
Expense claims	6 years after audit	Limitation Act 1980
Redundancy payments	6 years after payment	Limitation Act 1980
Accounts required under Section 221 of the Companies Act 1985	Private company – 3 years from date on which made Public company – 6 years from date on which made	Companies Act 1985 (subject also to Section 411 of the Insolvency Act 1986)

| Donations – all types | Current year plus 6 years | Tax management acts and the Limitation Act 1980 |
| Bank instruction | 6 years after ceasing to be effective | Limitation Act 1980 |

Cash records

Category	Retention period	Notes
Bank paying in counterfoils	6 years – unless cross-checked with statement, then 3 years	Companies Act 1985 and Limitation Act 1980
Bank statements	Public limited company – 6 years	Companies Act 1985 and Limitation Act 1980
Bank reconciliation	Limited company – 3 years	Companies Act 1985 and Limitation Act 1980
Banking returns	Date of return plus 6 years	Limitation Act 1980
Petty cash records	Current year plus 6 years	Limitation Act 1980
Main cash book	6 years after audit	Limitation Act 1980
Cash received sheets	Current year plus 6 years	Limitation Act 1980

Loan record

Category	Retention period	Notes
Debtor accounts control report	Date of report plus 6 years	Limitation Act 1980
Arrears schedule	Date of schedule plus 6 years	Limitation Act 1980
Individual debtor accounts	6 years after clearance of debt	Limitation Act 1980
Listing of wage deductions	Date of listing plus 3 years	Audit
Statement of loan account	Date of statement plus 6 years	Commercial practice

Pensions

Category	Retention period	Notes
Trust deeds and rules	Until fund ceases or merges plus 12 years	Taxes Management Act 1970, Limitation Act 1980 and Pensions Act 2004
Minute books	Until fund ceases or merges plus 12 years	Taxes Management Act 1970 and Limitation Act 1980
Pension payments	6 years after last payment of benefits	Taxes Management Act 1970 and Limitation Act 1980
Members' records	Review every 10 years	Audit and Data Protection Act 1998
Valuation working papers	Review every 10 years	Audit
Actuarial certificates	Review every 10 years	Audit

Superannuation adjustments	Current year plus 6 years	Taxes Management Act 1970 and Limitation Act 1980
Superannuation reports	Current year plus 6 years	Taxes Management Act 1970 and Limitation Act 1980

Salaries and wages

Category	Retention period	Notes
Tax forms P6/P45/P48/P11/P11D/P35/P60	At least 3 years after the end of the tax year to which they apply. Originals must be retained in paper or electronic format. Employees are required to retain their copies for 22 months after the current tax year.	Inland Revenue Booklet 490 refers
Payroll and salary records	6 years after audit	Taxes Management Act 1970, Limitation Act 1980 and Data Protection Act 1998
NI contributions	Current year plus 6 years	Taxes Management Act 1970 and Limitation Act 1980
Monthly superannuation	Current year plus 6 years	Taxes Management Act 1970 and Limitation Act 1980
Annual superannuation	Current year plus 6 years	Taxes Management Act 1970 and Limitation Act 1980
Annual earnings summary	Current year plus 6 years	Taxes Management Act 1970 and Limitation Act 1980

Sales records

Category	Retention period	Notes
Customer orders	3 to 6 years	Commercial practice
Customer complaints	3 months + depending on organization	Commercial practice
Nominal and private ledgers	Current year plus 10 years	Limitation Act 1980
Sales ledger	Current year plus 10 years	Limitation Act 1980
Sales invoices/credit notes	Current year plus 6 years	Taxes Management Act 1970 and Limitation Act 1980
Customer files	10 years after last entry	Limitation Act 1980. Note that some EU Directives specify 10 years
Delivery documentation	Current year plus 2 years	Audit

Health and safety

Category	Retention period	Notes
Accident books	3 years from date of last entry	Health and Safety (First Aid) Regulations 1981 Social Security (Claims and Payments) Regulations 1979 Social Security Administration Act 1992

Category	Retention period	Notes
Equipment inspection records	Varies according to equipment	Various Statutory Instruments
Geotechnical assessment of quarry	At least 3 years from date record was made	The Quarries Regulations 1999
Copy of declaration of EC conformity including final inspection certificate	10 years from date when safety component was last manufactured	Various EU Directives and Statutory Instruments
Asbestos (health records)	5 years from date of monitoring or 40 years if health record required	Control of Asbestos at Work Regulations 2002
Radioactivity (monitoring results)	2 years from the date on which they were made	Ionising Radiation Regulations 1999
Radioactivity (dose assessment and recording of classified person [approved dosimetry service])	Until the person to which it relates has or would have reached 75 but for at least 50 years from the date made	Ionising Radiation Regulations 1999
Control of substances hazardous to health (COSHH)	40 years from date of last incident	Control of Substances Hazardous to Health Regulations 2002
RIDDOR reports	3 years from date of notification	Reporting of Injuries, Diseases and Dangerous Occurrences Regulations 1995
Risk assessments	Until superseded (should be reviewed at a maximum of 3 years – earlier if circumstances change)	Management of Health and Safety at Work Regulations 1999

Safe systems of work	At least 6 months after completion of work	Commercial practice
Permit to work systems	A minimum of 12 months	Commercial practice
Compressed air health records	40 years from date of last entry	Work in Compressed Air Regulations 1996
Lifting operations – thorough examinations	For as long as equipment is operated	Lifting Operations and Lifting Equipment Regulations 1998
Machine maintenance books	Life of equipment	Workplace, Health, Safety and Welfare Approved Code of Practice Supply of Machinery (Safety) Regulations 1992
Construction – agents' written declaration	Life of health and safety file	Construction (Design and Management) Regulations 1994
Gas maintenance of residential properties	2 years from date of check	Gas Safety (Installation and Use) (Amendment) Regulations 1998
Statements/policies/ guides	Annual review	Commercial practice

Insurance

Category	Retention period	Notes
Policies	3 years after lapse	Commercial practice
Public/employers'/ product liability	Until superseded	Commercial practice

Claims correspondence	3 years after settlement	Commercial practice
Settlements	7 years after claim	Limitation Act 1980
Infant settlements	Until 24th birthday (in some cases infants are able to place a claim up to 6 years after their 18th birthday)	Limitation Act 1980
Insurance schedules	10 years after schedule expires	Commercial practice

Legal

Category	Retention period	Notes
Contracts/agreements under seal	12 years after expiry	Limitation Act 1980
Contracts/agreements – Other	6 years after expiry	Limitation Act 1980
Major agreements	Consider archiving for research	Commercial practice
Trademarks	Review at regular intervals	Commercial practice
Expired patents	12 years after expiry	Limitation Act 1980
Leases	12 years after expiry of lease	Limitation Act 1980
Planning permission	12 years after property interest ceased	Limitation Act 1980
Architect/builder agreements	6/12 years after contract end (see Contracts)	Limitation Act 1980
Title deeds	Until transferred to purchaser	Limitation Act 1980

Transport

Category	Retention period	Notes
Drivers' record books	Not less than 12 months	Transport Act 1968 Drivers' Hours (Goods Vehicles) (Keeping of Records) Regulations 1987
MOT test records	2 years after vehicle disposed of	Commercial practice
Mileage records	2 years after vehicle disposed of	Commercial practice
Vehicle maintenance records	2 years after vehicle disposed of	Commercial practice
Tachograph records	12 months after day of use	Transport Act 1968 EC Regulation 3821/85 Passenger and Goods Vehicles (Recording Equipment) Regulations 2005

Appendix G – Guidance on the Freedom of Information Act 2000

The Public Records Office publishes model action plans in connection with the Freedom of Information Act 2000, to help companies achieve compliance with the Lord Chancellor's Code of Practice relating to the Act. These plans note that a retention schedule is required in order to ensure retention and destruction decisions can be explained by documentation of the appraisal of records.

Note that even sticky notes and compliment slips may or may not have relevant information on them. On their own they may mean nothing but when read with the relevant information they could take on some importance. A report may be beneficial to its subject but a sticky note from the CEO saying the contents are a load of rubbish puts a different light on it! Such a note if detached and not mentioning the report by name is meaningless.

Extract from the Lord Chancellor's Code of Practice on the Management of Records under section 46 of the Freedom of Information Act 2000

5.1 The records management function should be recognised as a specific corporate programme within an authority and should receive the necessary levels of organisational support to ensure effectiveness. It should bring together responsibilities for records in all formats, including electronic records, throughout their lifecycle from planning and creation through to ultimate disposal. It should have clearly defined responsibilities and objectives, and the resources to achieve them. It is desirable that the person, or persons, responsible for the records management function should also have either direct responsibility or an organisational connection with the person or persons responsible for freedom of information, data protection and other information management issues.

Extract from the Freedom of Information (Scotland) Act 2002

Code of Practice on Records Management

4. Records management should be recognised as a specific corporate function within the authority and should receive the necessary levels of organisational support to ensure effectiveness. It should bring together responsibilities for **all** <u>records</u> held by the authority, throughout their lifecycle, from planning and creation through to ultimate <u>disposition</u>. It should have clearly defined responsibilities and objectives, and the resource to achieve them. It is desirable that the person, or persons, responsible for the records management function should also have either direct responsibility for, or a formal working relationship with, the person(s) responsible for: freedom of information, data protection and other information management issues. Authorities should prepare a records management strategy to support and guide the function.

Deleting electronic information

The following extract from an Information Tribunal appeal illustrates the Tribunal's view on when 'deleted' electronic information is or is not deleted from an organization's system from the point of the view of the Freedom of Information Act 2000.

Information Tribunal Appeal Number: EA/2005/0001

http://www.informationtribunal.gov.uk/our_decisions/documents/harper_v_information_commissioner.pdf

Between PAUL HARPER Appellant

And

THE INFORMATION COMMISSIONER Respondent

and

ROYAL MAIL Group PLC

Extract.

Deleted information

16. A very interesting matter arises from this case and that is the position of deleted electronic records. If a public authority has information that

has previously been held on a computer, but has been deleted, does that in itself mean that the information no longer comes within the scope of the Act. It is helpful here to go back to section 1 of the Act. An applicant's entitlement under section 1(1) is firstly to be informed in writing by the public authority whether it holds information of a specified description and if so, secondly, to have that information communicated to him. Both these rights relate to information that is held by the public authority. That then raises the question of what is meant by 'held' and the Act only gives limited help here. Section 3(2) states that 'For the purposes of this Act, information is held by a public authority if (a) it is held by the authority, otherwise and on behalf of another person, or (b) it is held by another person on behalf of the authority.' So that does not help with the specific problem about information that has been deleted from a computer. There is also the definition of 'information' in section 84 of the Act. Information, subject to two exceptions that do not apply here, 'means information recorded in any form'. So into section 1(1), where it refers to information, can be read the words 'recorded information'.

17. The Act plainly does envisage that there can be circumstances where information is held at one time, but not held at the time that the request is received. This is clear from the wording of section 1(4). The information to which the duties apply under the Act is the information in question held at the time when 'the request is received, except that account may be taken of any amendment or deletion between that time and the time when information is to be communicated under section 1(b) of the Act, being an amendment or deletion that would have been made regardless of the receipt of the request.' What that means is that in some cases information could be held when the request is received, but no longer appear to be held at the time when the request falls to be complied with. If it is no longer held because it has been deleted in the ordinary course of business, then the public authority can take account of this fact and may be able to say we no longer hold that information, subject to what we have to say below. So if, for example, there is a computer database which as a matter of routine is completely erased every six months, and the request is made on 1st January, and the six monthly erasure happens on 10th January, and the time for compliance expires in late January, it is possible to take account of that deletion. But if on receiving a request a public authority decides to delete relevant information, within the period of 20 working days within which a response must be made, such deletion would not be in the ordinary course of business and would be unlawful. For the purpose of considering the matter of deleted information, it is helpful to note that section 1(4) recognises the possibility that information could be held at one time, but not at another.

18. However section 1(4) says 'that account *may* be taken of any amendment or deletion' (word in italics our emphasis) and not that it <u>must</u> be taken into account and the applicant provided with the amended version, or no information where deleted by the time when the information is to be communicated to the applicant. The Tribunal interprets this as meaning that where the deleted or unamended information is still readily accessible and this is the information that the applicant wants, then the deleted or original version of the information should be recovered and that is what should be communicated to the applicant, with perhaps an explanation of what has happened to the information since the request was received.

19. Having said this the Tribunal takes the view that an authority which has routinely deleted information before a request is made should not be in a worse position than an authority that deletes information, in the normal course of business, after a request is made.

20. Against this background it is still necessary to consider the question: if a public authority has information that has been deleted from computer records is it still held? The Tribunal understands that information which is held electronically and then deleted (and even emptied later from a 'recycle bin' or 'trash can') is in fact still retained in its original form on the computer system until it is subsequently and actually overwritten by other information. In other words, information may be 'deleted' and 'emptied' but it is not actually eliminated from the system at that point. This is the case with most computer systems today, although no two systems will be identical, in terms of their treatment of deleted material. It will thus be a matter of fact and degree, depending on the circumstances of the individual case, whether potentially recoverable information is still held, for the purposes of the Act.

21. In view of the Tribunal's finding on the definition of information earlier in this decision, it may be incumbent on a Public Authority to make attempts to retrieve deleted information. Accordingly, the authority should establish whether information is completely eliminated, or merely deleted. In the latter case, the authority should consider whether the information can be recovered and if so by what means. There is computer software available that can be used to recover information that has been deleted from a computer system. If information has been deleted but can be recovered by various technical means, is that information still held by the public authority? The Tribunal finds that the answer to this question will be a matter of fact and degree depending on the circumstances of the individual case.

Methods to recover data

22. The actual methods which can be employed to recover data vary both in name and practice from one system to another, but broadly the Tribunal understands that the methods by which recovery can be achieved reasonably easily are as follows.

23. Firstly, systems can be restored entirely to a previous state using software that is part of the computer's own operating system. For example, the RESTORE facility in WINDOWS will restore the system to the way it existed on a previous date chosen by the operator, including information that existed at that date.

24. A second method involves 'backup' tapes. Networked systems will be 'backed up' using tapes, i.e. recording tapes that are made at intervals which preserve the state of the entire system at the chosen time. These can in principle be searched for information which was deleted after the time at which the tape was recorded. These tapes are usually recycled and re-recorded after a certain specified time, after which recovery of the original information from a tape would generally no longer be possible.

25. A third method involves 'Un-delete' or 'Recovery' which is a readily available process which uses special software, but commercially available in a large number of programmes, to search a disk or other medium to find deleted data tracks which remain on the disk but are not as yet overwritten, as described above. These programs operate by finding all such tracks of recorded information on the disk and then matching up tracks one with another to put the information file back together and bring it into view.

26. It is, of course, desirable that such procedures are carried out by IT personnel who have relevant experience as otherwise material which was added after the date chosen for restoration may be lost.

27. In a situation where deleted but not eliminated information exists and an undeleted version also exists, it will be necessary to consider which should be subject to disclosure. This would also apply to a situation where no undeleted version exists but where there are multiple deleted versions that can be recovered. In general, the version that was extant at the time at which the request was received should be supplied, save that an authority may wish to take account of any subsequent amendment, as provided for in s.1(4) of the Act.

How far should a public authority have to go to retrieve data?

28. The extent of the measures that could reasonably be taken by a Public Authority to recover deleted data will be a matter of fact and degree in each individual case. Simple restoration from a 'trash can' or 'recycle bin' folder, or from a back-up tape, should normally be attempted, as the Tribunal considers that such information continues to be held. Any attempted restoration that would involve the use of specialist staff time, or the use of specialist software, would have cost implications, which could be significant. In that event, the exemption arising from exceeding the 'appropriate limit', set from time to time under Section 12 of the Act, might be relied upon by an authority. Also it is relevant that the 20 day time limit itself gives an indication of the period for which an authority should strive diligently to comply with a request.

29. The Information Commissioner should give serious consideration to issuing guidance to Public Authorities on this matter, and to enquiring himself, where appropriate, in relation to complaints made to him, whether an authority has considered the recovery of deleted material.

Date: 14/11/2005   John Angel Chairman

End of extract

Appendix H – Electronic communications

Electronic communication is now part of everyday life. But can it be used for legal transactions? The answer is yes – providing specific legislation allows it.

The Electronic Communication Act 2003 defined 'in writing' as meaning 'in electronic format' or 'kept on a computer'.

The following are examples of government definitions of electronic communication as laid down in legislation. However, they are not always consistent or clear. If relying on a piece of legislation you should consult a legal source to ensure that it is the correct legislation and you are using it appropriately.

Extract from Statutory Instrument 2005 No. 2115, The Town and Country Planning (Major Infrastructure Project Inquiries Procedure) (England) Rules 2005

Electronic communications

3. —(1) In these Rules, and in relation to the use of electronic communications for any purpose of these Rules which is capable of being carried out electronically—

    a) the expression 'address' includes any number or address used for the purposes of such communications, except that where any provision of these Rules require any person to provide a name and address to any other person, the requirement shall not be fulfilled unless the person subject to the requirement provides a postal address;

    b) references to statements, notices, or other documents, or to copies of such documents, include references to such documents or copies of them in electronic form.

(2) Paragraphs (3) to (7) apply where an electronic communication is used by a person for the purpose of fulfilling any requirement of these Rules to give or send any statement, notice or other document to any other person ('the recipient').

(3) The requirement shall be taken to be fulfilled where the statement, notice or other document transmitted by means of the electronic communication is:

a) capable of being accessed by the recipient;

b) legible in all material respects; and

c) sufficiently permanent to be used for subsequent reference.

(4) In paragraph (3), 'legible in all material respects' means that the information contained in the statement, notice or document is available to the recipient to no lesser extent than it would be if sent or given by means of a document in printed form.

(5) Where the electronic communication is received by the recipient outside the recipient's business hours, it shall be taken to have been received on the next working day; and for this purpose 'working day' means a day which is not a Saturday, Sunday, Bank Holiday or other public holiday.

(6) A requirement of these Rules that any document shall be in writing is fulfilled where that document satisfies the criteria in paragraph (3).

(7) A requirement in these Rules to send more than one copy of a statement, notice or other document may be complied with by sending one copy only of the statement, notice or other document in question.

(8) Where a person is no longer willing to accept the use of electronic communications for any purpose of these Rules which is capable of being effected electronically, he shall give notice in writing—

(a) withdrawing any address notified to the Secretary of State or to a local planning authority for that purpose, or

(b) revoking any agreement entered into with the Secretary of State or with a local planning authority for that purpose,

and such withdrawal or revocation shall be final and shall take effect on a date specified by the person in the notice being not less than seven days after the date on which the notice is given.

End of extract

Editor's note

- A postal address still has to be given.

- Any references to documents or copies allows them to be sent in electronic formats.

- The requirement is fulfilled providing that the communication is capable of being accessed by the recipient; is legible in all material respects and is sufficiently permanent to be used for subsequent reference.

- If received outside normal hours, the electronic communication is deemed to have been received on the next working day.

- A requirement 'to be in writing' is met if the contents of paragraph 3 are met.

- If multiple copies are required only one copy has to be sent electronically.

- A change of mind over accepting an electronic communication requires positive action to be taken.

Here we have another extract – again from official legislation but note the differences.

Extract from Statutory Instrument 2005 No. 2045, The Income Tax (Construction Industry Scheme) Regulations 2005

Whether information has been delivered electronically

39. For the purpose of these Regulations, information is taken to have been delivered to an official computer system by an approved method of electronic communications only if it is accepted by that official computer system.

Proof of content of electronic delivery

40. —(1) A document certified by an officer of Revenue and Customs to be a printed-out version of any information delivered by an approved method of electronic communications is evidence, unless the contrary is proved, that the information—

a) was delivered by an approved method of electronic communications on that occasion, and

b) constitutes everything which was delivered on that occasion.

(2) A document which purports to be a certificate given in accordance with paragraph (1) is presumed to be such a certificate unless the contrary is proved.

Proof of identity of person sending or receiving electronic delivery

41. The identity of—

a) the person sending any information by an approved method of electronic communications to Her Majesty's Revenue and Customs, or

b) the person receiving any information delivered by an approved method of electronic communications by Her Majesty's Revenue and Customs,

is presumed, unless the contrary is proved, to be the person recorded as such on an official computer system.

Information sent electronically on behalf of a person

42. —(1) Any information delivered by an approved method of electronic communications—

a) to Her Majesty's Revenue and Customs, or

b) to an official computer system,

on behalf of a person is taken to have been delivered by that person.

(2) But this does not apply if the person proves that the information was delivered without the person's knowledge or connivance.

Proof of delivery of information sent electronically

43. —(1) The use of an approved method of electronic communications is presumed, unless the contrary is proved, to have resulted in the delivery of information—

a) to Her Majesty's Revenue and Customs, if the delivery of the information has been recorded on an official computer system;

b) by Her Majesty's Revenue and Customs, if the despatch of the information has been recorded on an official computer system.

(2) The use of a method of electronic communications is presumed, unless the contrary is proved, not to have resulted in the delivery of information—

a) to Her Majesty's Revenue and Customs, if the delivery of the information has not been recorded on an official computer system;

b) by Her Majesty's Revenue and Customs, if despatch of the information has not been recorded on an official computer system.

(3) The time of receipt or despatch of any information delivered by a method of electronic communications is presumed, unless the contrary is proved, to be the time recorded on an official computer system.

Proof of payment sent electronically

44. —(1) The use of a method of electronic communications is presumed, unless the contrary is proved, to have resulted in the making of a payment—

a) to Her Majesty's Revenue and Customs, if the making of the payment has been recorded on an official computer system;

b) by Her Majesty's Revenue and Customs, if despatch of the payment has been recorded on an official computer system.

(2) The use of a method of electronic communications is presumed, unless the contrary is proved, not to have resulted in the making of a payment:

a) to Her Majesty's Revenue and Customs, if the making of the payment has not been recorded on an official computer system;

b) by Her Majesty's Revenue and Customs, if despatch of the payment has not been recorded on an official computer system.

(3) The time of receipt or despatch of any payment sent by a method of electronic communications is presumed, unless the contrary is proved, to be the time recorded on an official computer system.

Mandatory electronic payment

45. —(1) If an e-payment notice has been issued to a contractor in respect of a tax year under regulation 199 of the PAYE Regulations, he must pay the specified payment using an approved method of electronic communications.

(2) Paragraph (1) applies regardless of whether a payment of tax is due under regulation 68 of the PAYE Regulations (payment and recovery of tax by employer).

(3) If the Commissioners for Her Majesty's Revenue and Customs have given directions under regulation 199(3) of the PAYE Regulations

in relation to a contractor, the specified payment must be made in accordance with those directions.

End of extract.

A third example follows.

Extract from Statutory Instrument 2006 No. 237, The Non-Domestic Rating and Council Tax (Electronic Communications) (England) Order 2006

The First Secretary of State makes the following Order in exercise of the powers conferred by section 8 of the Electronic Communications Act 2000[1].

The First Secretary of State considers that the authorisation of the use of electronic communications by this Order for any purpose is such that the extent (if any) to which records of things done for that purpose will be available will be no less satisfactory in cases where use is made of electronic communications or electronic storage than in other cases.

Citation, commencement and application

1. This Order, which applies to England only[2], may be cited as the Non-Domestic Rating and Council Tax (Electronic Communications) (England) Order 2006 and shall come into force on 1st March 2006.

Amendment of the Non-Domestic Rating (Collection and Enforcement) (Central Lists) Regulations 1989

2. The Non-Domestic Rating (Collection and Enforcement) (Central Lists) Regulations 1989[3] are amended in accordance with articles 3 and 4.

3. In regulation 2(1) insert—

   a)   after the definition of 'the 1993 Act'—

   '"address" in relation to electronic communications includes any number or address used for the purposes of such communications;';

   b)   after the definition of 'the amount payable'—

   '"business day" means any day except a Saturday or Sunday, Christmas Day, Good Friday or a day which is a bank holiday under the Banking and Financial Dealings Act 1971 in England and Wales;'[4]; and

c) after the definition of 'demand notice'—

'"electronic communication" means a communication transmitted (whether from one person to another, from one device to another or from a person to a device or vice versa)—

a) by means of an electronic communications network within the meaning of section 32(1) of the Communications Act 2003;

b) by other means but while in an electronic form;' [5].

4. For regulation 3 substitute—

'Service of notices

3. —(1) Any notice required or authorised by these Regulations to be served on a person by the Secretary of State may be served—

a) in the case of a body corporate, by addressing the notice or information to the secretary of the body and:

   i) delivering it to him,

   ii) leaving it at or by sending it by post to him at the registered or principal office of the body, or

   iii) sending it to him by electronic communication to such address as may be notified by him for that purpose; and

b) in any other case, by:

   i) delivering the notice or information to the person,

   ii) leaving it at or sending it by post to him at his last place of abode or an address given by him at which service will be accepted, or

   iii) sending it to him by electronic communication to such an address as may be notified by him for that purpose.

(2) For the purpose of any legal proceedings, a notice given by the means described in paragraph (1)(a)(iii) or (b)(iii) shall, unless the contrary is proved, be treated as served on the second business day after it was sent.

(3) A person who has notified an address for the purpose of paragraph (1)(a)(iii) or (b)(iii) shall, by notice in writing to the Secretary of State, advise the Secretary of State of any change in that address; and the change shall take effect on the third business day after the date on which the notice is received by the Secretary of State.

(4) A person who has notified an address for the purpose of paragraph (1)(a)(iii) or (b)(iii) may, by notice in writing to the Secretary of State, withdraw that notification; and the withdrawal shall take effect on the third business day after the date on which the notice is received by the Secretary of State.

(5) Where a company registered outside the United Kingdom has an office in the United Kingdom, that office shall be treated for the purpose of paragraph (1)(a)(ii) as its principal office; and where it has more than one office in the United Kingdom its principal office in the United Kingdom shall be treated as its principal office for that purpose.'

Amendment of the Non-Domestic Rating (Collection and Enforcement) (Local Lists) Regulations 1989

5. The Non-Domestic Rating (Collection and Enforcement) (Local Lists) Regulations 1989[6] are amended in regulation 1(2), by the substitution, for the definition of 'electronic communication', of—

'"electronic communication" means a communication transmitted (whether from one person to another, from one device to another or from a person to a device or vice versa)—

 a) by means of an electronic communications network within the meaning of section 32(1) of the Communications Act 2003;

 b) by other means but while in an electronic form;'.

Amendment of the Council Tax (Administration and Enforcement) Regulations 1992

6. The Council Tax (Administration and Enforcement) Regulations 1992[7] are amended in regulation 1(2), by the substitution, for the definition of 'electronic communication', of—

'"electronic communication" means a communication transmitted (whether from one person to another, from one device to another or from a person to a device or vice versa)—

 a) by means of an electronic communications network within the meaning of section 32(1) of the Communications Act 2003;

 b) by other means but while in an electronic form;'.

EXPLANATORY NOTE

(This note is not part of the Order)

Articles 2 to 4 of this Order amend the Non-Domestic Rating (Collection and Enforcement) (Central Lists) Regulations 1989 ('the Central Lists Regulations') in relation to England. They provide for the service by the Secretary of State of certain notices by means of electronic communication where the recipient has agreed to accept electronic service.

Article 3 inserts new definitions into regulation 2 of the Central Lists Regulations and article 4 replaces existing regulation 3. New regulation 3(1) allows the notices which are required to be served by the Secretary of State (in particular demand notices under regulation 4 and further demand notices under regulation 8) to be served electronically. If a ratepayer does not specify an address for electronic service, he will continue to receive notices in paper form. Paragraphs (3) and (4) of new regulation 3 provide that the recipient of electronic notices must notify the Secretary of State in writing of any change in his electronic address and that he may withdraw his agreement to accepting electronic service.

Articles 5 and 6 amend the Non-Domestic Rating (Collection and Enforcement) (Local Lists) Regulations 1989 and the Council Tax (Administration and Enforcement) Regulations 1992 to reflect the definition of 'electronic communication' in section 15 of the Electronic Communications Act 2000.

End of extract.

Some very wordy descriptions of electronic communication, and there are others! They all differ according to the main subject of the legislation. So it is not safe to assume that all information sent or received electronically is the master or legal copy unless it meets the exact criteria of the legislation to which it relates.

Email

Having discussed electronic communication, what is email? Email is just the 'envelope' that the electronic communication arrives in. Just as if the information had arrived in an envelope it needs to be opened, read and actioned.

Email may be:

- read and thrown away;
- read and replied to;

- read and filed;

- read, actioned and filed.

When filing email, the information should be treated in the same way as other formats. Use the style of file and title and ensure the metadata is sufficient to enable the information to be easily and quickly retrieved. If this action is not followed then it becomes difficult to find the information again and it may be missed during information audits or retention checks. If the system allows it, the retention period should be entered at the time of creation, receipt or filing.

Saving emails in inboxes until deleted because of lack of space is not managing information efficiently. If electronic information is to be retained then steps have to be taken not only to ensure it can be retrieved quickly and easily at a suitable cost but also to ensure it does not get corrupted or altered. Readers are therefore advised to read BIP 0008:2004, *Legal admissibility and evidential weight of information stored electronically* and PD ISO/TR 18492:2005, *Long-term preservation of electronic document-based information.*

Conservatively, up to 50% of personal e-mail can be classified as spam or at least unsolicited. The size of the problem has been put into perspective by the projection that we will reach a level in excess of 36 billion emails per day during 2005, a three-fold increase in six years (*Computer Weekly*, November 2004).

A growing amount of an organisation's business and intellectual records is contained in e-mail, often locked in personal folders which are normally only accessible to the originator and/or the recipient. According to industry analysts, up to 60% of organisations consider e-mail to be a mission-critical application, and up to 60% of business-critical information resides in messaging systems.

Source: *Records Management Society Bulletin*, Issue 126, p.51.

Examples of emails causing problems in court

United Insurance v. Unisys (2001)

In a High Court action the judge commented, 'One thing that one learns from this case is the trap that emails can lead you into.' An insurance company was claiming a £14 million refund from its technology supplier.

A number of internal emails, between project team members and their management, had been presented in court. The implications from the emails were that the technology supplier was well aware of the problems that eventually led to the cancellation of the project. The supplier argued in court that the emails used deliberately strong language in a bid to get a response from management. Employees had made claims that they might not have, had they had more information.

Source: *Computer Weekly*, 5 July 2001

Insurance company: United Insurance

Technology supplier: Unisys

Journalist: Tony Collins

US Department of Justice v. Microsoft (1999)

In its antitrust trial against Microsoft the US Department of Justice repeatedly introduced email evidence that was damaging to the company. In this example, David Boies, the government's lead attorney in the case, introduced the email to rebut a portion of the written direct testimony of Microsoft's first witness, Richard Schmalensee, dean of the Sloan School of Management at the Massachusetts Institute of Technology.

Boies asked Schmalensee whether the poll had more to do with giving Microsoft chairman Bill Gates a favourable position going into a Senate hearing on competition in the software industry the previous March. Senator Orrin Hatch had invited Gates and several other leading computer and software company executives to the hearing.

Schmalensee said he was not aware of a connection between the poll and the Senate hearing.

However, in a 14 February 1998 email written by Gates to some of the company's top executives and attorneys, the Microsoft CEO wrote: 'I want to get a survey done where ISVs [independent software vendors] declare whether they think having the browser in the operating system the way we are planning to do it makes sense and is good. It would help me immensely to have a survey showing that 90 per cent of developers believe that putting the browser into the OS [operating system] makes sense. Ideally, we would have a survey like this done before I appear at the Senate on March 3rd.'

Nathan Myhrvold, Microsoft's chief technology officer, and one of the recipients of Gates' email, wrote back on 15 February 1998: 'Saying "put the browser in the OS" is already a statement that is prejudicial to us. The name "browser" suggests a separate thing. I would not phrase the survey, or other things only in terms of "put the browser in the OS".'

'Instead,' Myhrvold continued, 'you need to ask a more neutral question about how internet technology needs to merge with local computing. I have been pretty successful in trying this on various journalists and industry people.'

Mark Murray, a spokesman for Microsoft, said the company did have a third-party organization conduct such a survey, polling some 200 developers on their views. Murray also cited other parts of the Gates email, one of which said, 'We have never put crazy stuff into the OS and it's time for people to know we are doing this for developers and customers.'

Gates' email also suggested several well-known names in the industry that he hoped would sign up to Microsoft's plans, including Novell CEO Eric Schmidt, Intuit CEO Scott Cook, Symantec CEO Gordon Eubanks and industry pundit Esther Dyson.

Microsoft executive Ann Redmond wrote an email dated 23 February 1998, which responded to the survey issue and its results. But Redmond said, 'I wouldn't refer to it as unbiased, and wouldn't refer to it as an opinion poll.' Redmond then gave some examples of unbiased approaches.

Ironically, Microsoft then issued a press release announcing an independent poll showed that 73 per cent of Americans believed Microsoft had benefited both US consumers and the computer software industry.

AIIM Information

Source: Computer Reseller News http://www.crn.com/

Journalist: Darryl K Taft

Appendix I – Sources of information

Websites

While many higher education establishments allow access to their retention schedules via their websites, private companies tend to be reluctant to release any details, claiming business confidentiality.

Higher education example

Joint Information Systems Committee (JISC) records retention in further education resource

This release gives a generic records retention schedule that can be adopted and used by institutions in the further education sector.

This resource adopts the same functional approach as its predecessor, making it applicable to the full range of further education institutions.

Enhancements to the current version include:

- an improved layout;

- cross-references to the Higher Education Records Retention Schedule;

- cross-references to relevant entries in both the UK and Scottish Model Publication Schemes;

- an internal search engine;

- a downloadable version of the database's contents in Microsoft Excel format for repurposing within an institution.

The Records Retention in Further Education Resource is available from http://www.jiscinfonet.ac.uk/projects/records-retention-fe/index_html

Batchelor Associates

For advice and guidance on retention periods and schedules.
http://surf.to/keith.batchelor

Her Majesty's Stationery Office website

To view and download legislation (see notes on website regarding Crown Copyright).
http://www.opsi.gov.uk/

The Stationery Office website

To order paper copies of legislation.
http://www.tso.co.uk/

Records Management Society of Great Britain

For advice and guidance on records management issues.
http://www.rms-gb.org.uk/

Society of Archivists

For advice and guidance on archival matters.
http://www.archives.org.uk/

UKAIIM Standards Committee

For advice and guidance on records management issues.
http://www.ukaiim.org/

Glossary

appraisal

the act of reviewing information to see if it is under the correct classification, needs to be kept or destroyed, or needs to be migrated to a different format to protect or preserve the information

archive

store as a historical document for future research by the organization or others

archives

store containing historical documents

classification

means of dividing information into sets or series (usually by function or activity) to aid retrieval

NOTE: This involves the systematic identification and (usually hierarchical) arrangement of business activities, documents, records and folders into categories in order that records or information can be grouped together for efficient organization and retrieval.

destruction

process of eliminating or deleting records, beyond any possible reconstruction

disposal

process of moving or disposing of information

disposition

range of processes associated with implementing records retention, destruction or transfer decisions that are documented in disposition authorities and other instruments

document

often defined as 'any recorded information or object that can be treated as a unit of filing'

NOTE: Thus a letter, form or report can be considered a document. A record can be described as a record once it records activity. However, many documents exist in their own right. For example, an empty printed form is a document, whereas once it has been completed it can be registered as a record since its contents record an activity and give it added meaning.

Under the Criminal Justice Act 1988, Schedule 2 a document is defined as 'anything in which information of any description is recorded'.

folder

set of related electronic and/or physical records or information. They can be associated with metadata

indexing

process of establishing access points to facilitate retrieval of records and/or information

information

all retained information regardless of format – i.e. film (analogue or digital), paper, electronic (floppy disk, hard disk, CD-ROM or tape) or 'hard' information (e.g. rock samples, items from a scene of crime)

metadata

data describing the context, content and structure of the record(s) or information. It also describes their management through time

migration

act of moving information from one system to another, while maintaining the information's authenticity, integrity, reliability and usability

record

information created, received and maintained as evidence and information by an organization or person, in pursuance of legal obligations or in the transaction of business (from BS ISO 15489, *Records management*)

NOTE: Records can be any of the following:

* records created by the organization in the course of its business;
* 'public records' (e.g. records of courts, coroners, hospitals and prisons) held on behalf of central government;
* information given to or purchased by the organization or deposited with the organization – normally on indefinite loan.

A record should be able to support the needs of the business to which it relates and be used for accountability purposes.

retention schedule

programme of events for the keeping, disposition and disposal of records

transfer

change of custody, ownership and/or responsibility for the information. Can also mean moving records from one place to another

vital/prime

term usually used by those in records management to describe documents that if lost would cause loss of business or serious embarrassment

NOTE: Unfortunately this is usually translated by staff to mean their own work, as to them the information they look after is vital to the ease of carrying out their function in the organization. If the word 'prime' is used instead then very few items of information are identified. This makes it easier to protect the information that really needs it. Such information will be duplicated by back-ups such as copying to paper or electronic media and ideally stored in a separate location away from the building in which it is usually used.

weed

remove information from a file or record when that information is no longer required

Bibliography

BS 1467:1972, *Specification for folders and files*

BS 4783-1:1988, *Storage, transportation and maintenance of media for use in data processing and information storage — Part 1: Recommendations for disk packs, storage modules and disk cartridges*

BS 4783-2:1988, *Storage, transportation and maintenance of media for use in data processing and information storage — Part 2: Recommendations for magnetic tape on open spools*

BS 4783-3:1988, *Storage, transportation and maintenance of media for use in data processing and information storage — Part 3: Recommendations for flexible disk cartridges*

BS 4783-4:1988, *Storage, transportation and maintenance of media for use in data processing and information storage — Part 4: Recommendations for magnetic tape cartridges and cassettes*

BS 4783-5:1991, *Storage, transportation and maintenance of media for use in data processing and information storage — Part 5: Recommendations for 12.7 mm magnetic tape cartridges for data interchange, recording at 1491 data bytes per millimetre on 18 tracks*

BS 4783-6:1993, *Storage, transportation and maintenance of media for use in data processing and information storage — Part 6: Recommendations for optical disk cartridges (ODC)*

BS 4783-7:1993, *Storage, transportation and maintenance of media for use in data processing and information storage — Part 7: Recommendations for optical data disks (CD-ROM)*

BS 4783-8:1994, *Storage, transportation and maintenance of media for use in data processing and information storage — Part 8: Recommendations for 4 mm and 8 mm helical scan tape cartridges*

BS 5097-1:1974, *Specification for loose leaf binders — Part 1: Ring binders with metal mechanisms*

BS 5454:2000, *Recommendations for the storage and exhibition of archival documents*

BS 6529:1984, *Recommendations for examining documents, determining their subjects and selecting indexing terms*

BS 25999-1, *Code of practice for business continuity management*

BS ISO 15489-1:2001, *Information and documentation — Records management — Part 1: General*

BS ISO/IEC 17799:2005, *Information technology — Security techniques — Code of practice for information security management*

PD ISO/TR 18492:2005, *Long-term preservation of electronic document-based information*

BIP 0008-1:2004, *Legal admissibility and evidential weight of information stored electronically*

BIP 0009-1:2004, *Legal admissibility and evidential weight of information stored electronically – Compliance Workbook*

PD 0024:2001, *Archival documents — Guide to the interpretation of BS 5454:2001 — Storage and exhibition of archival documents*

PD ISO/TR 15489-2:2001, *Information and documentation — Records management — Part 2: Guidelines*